SPLENDID SALADS

Cooking Arts Collection™

About the Author

Kathleen Prisant cooks with a view of Pike Place Market in Seattle, Washington, and in the lush Sonoma Valley of California. She is a frequent contributor to *Cooking Pleasures* magazine. As contributing editor for *Diablo* magazine, she produced the monthly column "Local Flavor" and was President of the San Francisco Professional Food Society.

Food companies and wineries have employed her talents for recipe development, food styling, teaching and event planning for over twenty years. To augment her degree in Home Economics from University of California at Davis and courses at the Culinary Institute of America in the Napa Valley, Kathleen studied with leading food professionals in Tuscany, Provence, Oaxaca and Hanoi.

SPLENDID SALADS

Printed in 2008.

Tom Carpenter, Creative Director
Heather Koshiol, Managing Editor
Jennifer Weaverling, Production Editor
Julie Cisler, Senior Book Designer
Shari Gross, Production Designer
Laura Holle, Senior Book Development Assistant
Phil Aarrestad Photography, Commissioned Photography
Robin Krause, Food Stylist
Susan Telleen, Prop Stylist, Assistant Food Stylist

Special thanks to: Terry Casey, Janice Cauley, Pat Durkin, Elizabeth Gunderson, Cindy Jurgensen, Bea Krinke, Nancy Maurer, Mary Jo Myers, Ruth Petran and Martha Zeimer.

Cover: Shaved Beet Salad with Chardonnay Vinaigrette, page 75.
Page 1: Watermelon Salad, page 149.

5 6 7 8 / 10 09 08
© 2003 Cooking Club of America
ISBN 10: 1-58159-173-X
ISBN 13: 978-1-58159-173-6

Cooking Club of America
12301 Whitewater Drive
Minnetonka, MN 55343
www.cookingclub.com

TABLE OF CONTENTS

# INTRODUCTION

Anthropologists classify our early human ancestors as hunter-gatherers who ate a diet of meat they hunted and plant matter they gathered. Greens must have somehow worked their way into the "gathering" part of the mix and *voila* … the first salads were born!

Salad has come a long way. But not so long ago — think back, maybe even to your own childhood — mundane old iceberg lettuce was the mainstay of both family dinner and restaurant salads … if salad was on the menu at all. No wonder salad wasn't considered something to elevate and celebrate.

Today, thank goodness, we love a good salad … and appreciate the wonderful spectrum of forms that salad can take. Whether the occasion is a family weeknight

meal, a special weekend dinner, an entertaining occasion, even a friendly potluck or other large gathering … salad makes the menu, and makes the menu special.

And salad is so much more than just greens these days. Sure, greens are still a mainstay. But salad takes on a variety of other forms, shapes, tastes, looks and uses in the modern culinary world.

That's why we created *Splendid Salads* — to bring Cooking Club of America Members a wide and exciting selection of salads to choose from and add to their culinary repertoires. These ideas are for *you*.

Make new dressings to pair with salads you already like. Discover new green salads. Give the vegetable salads a test run.

Sometimes you're looking for heartier fare — maybe even a whole meal. That's where meat, fish and chicken salads come in. And try some of the pasta salad ideas, or the wonderful bean and grain salads, as side dishes.

Look for twists on sandwich salad traditions, as well as some all-new creations you'll want to make. Gather ideas for picnic salads that are "safe to take" and great to eat. And top off any meal with a light and refreshing fruit or dessert salad.

You can define *Splendid* any number of ways — glorious, superb, magnificent, excellent, grand, showy; likewise with *Salads* — greens, vegetables, beans, grains, pasta, meat, sandwiches, fruit.

Splendid Salads brings it all together for you!

SALAD ESSENTIALS

Part of salads' attraction is their simplicity. But those delicate interplays of flavor aren't just random. It takes some thinking, and some knowledge and planning, to create salads that make your taste buds sing. So here is some salad history. A glossary of greens. The tools you need. And the basics behind different kinds of dressings. With these salad essentials in hand, you'll be prepared to create some of the greatest salads of your life — right at home, where freshness and flavor are guaranteed.

LIFE WITH SALAD

"Eat just a bite of salad!" That was Mother's plea when we were merely exploring the possibility of eating something green. My, how we change. And how our concept of salad has changed too.

Even in California's great Central Valley farm country where I was raised, salad was iceberg lettuce and beefsteak tomatoes. I must confess that I still dream of those perfect beefsteak tomatoes, and I liked the iceberg lettuce and the thick, creamy bottled dressings. Bounty was part of life in our town; variety wasn't.

Greens may have been cultivated 4500 years ago, and even 3000 years ago they were thought to promote good health and digestion. Hippocrates espoused the health benefits of lettuce, and even then the question was whether to eat salad before or following a meal. Some said serving salad before the entrée encouraged the appetite. Proponents of serving salad following the meal assured diners that it would aid in digestion.

In North America, we generally eat our salad first. A restaurateur once told me that salad helps the customer pass time while the entrée is being prepared. I think he made that up. But eating salad as a first course seems to be our tradition. Many Europeans prefer their salad after the entrée.

Some cultures make no differentiation between the salad course and other courses. Many dishes that we consider salads are an integral part of the meal. Think of the tapas table, a groaning board of small dishes served as appetizers or as a complete meal. Salads of beans and herbs are served along with steamed garlicky mussels. Grilled vegetable salads are offered with cold tomato soup. In Vietnam, entrées look like salads. Steaming plates of fish are piled with fresh herbs, sprouts and greens.

But you should also think beyond the salad course to salad meals. Grains, beans, pasta and rice are the basis for hearty salads served as side dishes. Bits of chicken, meat and cheese turn almost any salad into an entrée. Include fruit in salads. As you'll see, fruit salads can work anywhere in a meal. They can even be a meal.

The Produce for Better Health Foundation and the National Cancer Institute recommend that every American eat five servings of fruit and vegetables every day for better health. A serving can be as small as one plum, a cup of mixed green salad or a quarter cup of dried fruit. Incorporating one big salad can easily provide you with two of your five servings per day.

When you are watching calories, salads can be perfect dieting food. But forgo the high-fat dressings and calorie-rich additions. Eat nuts, mayonnaise-based dressings and oil-soaked ingredients in moderation. Salads based on fresh ingredients, and lightly dressed, will fill you up, not out!

GLOSSARY OF GREENS

The term "greens" describes a huge category of leafy vegetables. When building green salads, we most often think of lettuces! Put some sturdy green vegetables that pleasantly make the transition from braised and stir-fried to raw in the salad bowl.

Across the country, our salad repertoire is growing, thanks to specialty farmers and expanding produce counters. Visit farmers' markets to seek out unfamiliar varieties of greens and keep adding to your list of favorites.

For the ultimate in salad greens, grow them from seed. A small plot or a few containers, good soil and mild temperatures create the right environment for experimenting with such diverse lettuces as Lolla Rossa and Tat Soi.

Storage time for greens is usually short. However, I've noticed a broad range of refrigerator life depending on how fresh the greens were when purchased. I often buy spring mix from a lady who harvests it each morning and sells it by the armloads. Fresh, washed and ready to serve, her greens last in the refrigerator for a week. I've purchased the same style of mix at the grocery store to have it die the next day.

ARUGULA

DESCRIPTION. Ranging from baby leaves with a pleasant peppery-tart bite, to large older leaves which can taste bitter, arugula has long been a salad staple in Europe. Tender baby arugula can be enjoyed with the stems left on. Remove stems from the larger leaves. Arugula is often added to spring mix (page 16).

USES. Arugula is delicious as the base of a green salad or in a mix. Vinaigrettes and soft goat cheese are particularly complementary. A few leaves tossed with pasta or in a bean salad lend a fresh, peppery bite. Choose baby arugula, if it's available.

PREPARATION. Remove stems from larger leaves. Thoroughly wash arugula in cool water and drain well. Spin or shake dry.

STORAGE. Spread out on a clean dish towel or paper towels. Roll up and store in a plastic bag in the refrigerator. Use within 4 days.

BOSTON LETTUCE

DESCRIPTION. This loose-leafed head lettuce is one of the butterhead varieties. Boston lettuce has a smooth, buttery texture. Bibb lettuce (limestone), similar but with a smaller head, is considered a gourmet treat.

USES. The delicately flavored leaves of Boston lettuce benefit from simple vinaigrettes such as white wine vinegar with Dijon mustard and a fruity olive oil.

PREPARATION. Remove leaves from the core. The leaves bruise easily, so wash whole leaves individually and pat dry.

STORAGE. Spread out on a clean dish towel or paper towels. Roll up and store in a plastic bag in the refrigerator. Use within 4 days.

CABBAGE — RED AND GREEN

DESCRIPTION. Although many varieties exist, our most common cabbage is the heavy, tightly packed red or white head. Other varieties include Chinese cabbage (see below), savoy cabbage and kale.

USES. This versatile vegetable withstands long cooking and can also be enjoyed raw, as in coleslaw (which means "cool cabbage"). Cabbage is most pleasant when shredded very thin and tossed with either a creamy dressing or vinaigrette. Its sturdiness stands up well to hot bacon dressing.

PREPARATION. Quarter the head of cabbage, cut out the core. Shred cabbage thinly using a sharp knife, mandoline or food processor. Wash, drain, then spin the shreds until dry.

STORAGE. Spread out on a clean dish towel or paper towels. Roll up and store in a plastic bag in the refrigerator. Use within 2 days. The head, kept whole, can be refrigerated for as long as a week.

CHINESE CABBAGE (NAPA CABBAGE)

DESCRIPTION. This pale green, crinkly cabbage is more tender than red or green cabbage. Look for clean, blemish-free, untorn heads.

USES. Chinese cabbage makes a delicate coleslaw when tossed with any number of vinaigrettes. It's also terrific in stir-fried dishes.

PREPARATION. Cut off the core end and cut the head in halves lengthwise. Then cut each half crosswise into thin shreds. Rinse the shreds and spin until dry.

STORAGE. Wrap the uncut head in paper towels and store in the vegetable bin in the refrigerator. For convenience, core, shred, wash and dry the cabbage, then wrap it in a plastic bag. Just reach into the bag for a handful of shreds to make a quick salad. It keeps for about 3 days.

ENDIVE

DESCRIPTION. This beautiful, tenderly cared-for vegetable is the sprout of the gnarled chicory root. It is grown indoors or under cover so it doesn't turn green. Choose very white endive, as it becomes bitter as it turns green.

USES. Whole leaves make elegant hors d'oeuvres for filling or for dipping. Whole leaves also make a lovely arranged salad. For use in tossed salads, stack leaves and cut into thin strips, either lengthwise or crosswise. Immediately toss the strips with dressing or in lemon juice to prevent browning.

PREPARATION. Just before serving, remove leaves from the core. Leaves bruise easily and turn brown when wet. Wipe the whole leaves individually and pat dry.

STORAGE. Wrap whole endives in paper towels or waxed paper; let breathe. Store in the refrigerator for up to 3 days.

FRISEE (CURLY ENDIVE)

DESCRIPTION. Frisee has it all: a pretty, lacy appearance, a slightly bitter and sweet flavor combination, and a crisp texture. Because it's pricey, it's often served at a dinner party rather than during a hectic family weeknight meal.

USES. Serve frisee as a base for a pretty salad with a berry vinaigrette and just one or two other ingredients. Fresh pears, toasted nuts and flavorful cheese all contrast nicely with this green. Frisee is often added to spring mix (page 16).

PREPARATION. Remove the core and largest stems. Gently wash and drain frisee in cool water. Shake or pat dry.

STORAGE. Spread out on a clean dish towel or paper towels; roll up. Store in a plastic bag in the refrigerator. Use within 3 days.

ICEBERG LETTUCE

DESCRIPTION.
"America's lettuce."
Iceberg is a crisphead
lettuce, meaning, it's a
large, tightly packed head
of crisp leaves. Sturdy and
refreshing, iceberg stands
up to creamy, flavorful
dressings. And it's one of
the few lettuces you can
cut with a knife, allowing
you to serve great piles of
shredded lettuce as a base
of all sorts of composed
salads.

USES. The crisp, refreshing character of iceberg lends itself to rich
"restaurant-style" dressings such as blue cheese, thousand island and ranch.
Serve iceberg shredded, torn or cut into wedges.

PREPARATION. Iceberg must be crisp, as it is after it has drawn a lot of
water into its cells. Rap the core on the counter, twist and remove. Plunge
the head into a bowl of cold water. Let it sit for about 5 minutes; drain well.
Then proceed with your recipe.

STORAGE. Drain and store the head of lettuce in a plastic bag. Or cut or
tear into bite-size pieces and store. Refrigerate and use within 1 week.

LEAF LETTUCE

DESCRIPTION. Leaf lettuce is a general category of lettuce whose leaves
branch out instead of forming a head. Bronze Leaf, Canasta, Green Leaf,
Green Oak, Lolla Rossa, Manoa, Red Leaf, Red Oak Leaf, Ruby, Red Leaf,
Tango — these are some of the many varieties we now see around the
country. While specialty markets carry one or two varieties, farmers'
markets are the best source for the more obscure greens.

USES. Combine these mild lettuces with more peppery leaves such as
mustard greens, mizuna and Tat Soi.

PREPARATION. Remove leaves from the core. Tear into bite-size pieces.
Wash and drain the leaves and shake out or spin dry.

STORAGE. Spread out on a clean dish towel or paper towels. Roll up and
store in plastic bag in the refrigerator. Use within 4 days.

ROMAINE (COS)

DESCRIPTION. Long loaves of romaine lettuce have deep green outer leaves and tender, pale inner leaves. Like iceberg, romaine lettuce is sturdy and crisp.

USES. The traditional Caesar salad green, romaine is as versatile as lettuce gets. It can be cut with a knife into shreds and chunks. The beautiful, long white leaves from its heart can grace an oversized plate. For an elegant Caesar, drizzle hearts of romaine with olive oil and lemon juice. Top with one or two anchovy filets, sprinkle with garlicky croutons and top with shavings of Parmesan.

PREPARATION. Cut off the end just above the core. Soak the head in cold water for about 5 minutes. Drain well.

STORAGE. Spread romaine out on a clean dish towel or paper towels. Roll up and store in plastic bag in the refrigerator. Use within 4 days.

SPINACH

DESCRIPTION. Spinach comes in a crinkled variety that's best for cooking and smooth varieties that are delicious in salads and cooked dishes. Baby spinach is the most tender, stems and all.

USES. Choose dark green, smooth small spinach leaves for making a salad. To soften the slightly bitter taste of spinach, add ingredients with a little fat, such as bacon, sliced hard-cooked eggs or toasted nuts.

PREPARATION. Like most delicate greens, spinach leaves bruise easily. Submerge in cold water, drain and repeat this process. Gently pat dry between clean towels. Remove the stems of large leaves. Enjoy baby spinach stem and all.

STORAGE. Washed and dried, spinach can be refrigerated for 3 to 4 days.

SPRING MIX (MESCLUN)

DESCRIPTION. We owe gratitude to the distributors of spring mix for introducing tender specialty greens to our kitchens. Many mixes include arugula, mache, frisee and one or two other field greens. Sometimes, a few herbs are added.

USES. Most mixes are in between delicate and sturdy, making them an all-purpose salad base. From basic lettuce and tomatoes to an upscale salad with Champagne vinaigrette and toasted hazelnuts, spring mix is a salad staple.

PREPARATION. Many of these mixes are sanitized and ready to eat. But rinsing them under cool water and spinning dry will make greens crisp and keep them fresh longer.

STORAGE. Wash, drained, dried and refrigerated in a plastic bag, fresh spring mix will last about 4 days.

WATERCRESS

DESCRIPTION. Watercress grows in cool running water. Its small, round leaves are dark green and crisp when it's fresh. The long stems are tender and can be left attached to the leaves, or you can use just the leaves in your salad.

USES. The lively, peppery flavor of watercress makes it a welcome addition to more mild greens, such as butter lettuce. It adds a nice bite to chicken salad sandwiches and is pretty floating on a creamy soup.

PREPARATION. Just before using, wash, drain, then spin or pat dry between clean towels or paper towels.

STORAGE. Snip off the root end of the stems and stand the bouquet of watercress in a glass of water in the refrigerator for up to 3 days.

$\mathcal{S}$ALAD TOOLS & TECHNIQUES

Kitchen tools can be as basic as a good set of knives, a cutting board, bowls and spoons. However, there are a few items that streamline cooking tasks. While you'll undoubtedly recognize most of the tools on the list, you may find some new uses for them.

Asian Bamboo Steamer Insert. A bamboo steamer (see photo), set over a wok of simmering water, is a terrific way to steam and flavor ingredients. Make sure you have a heatproof plate that will fit inside the steamer, so that herbs, spices, garlic, ginger and liquid ingredients can be steamed along with the main ingredient.

Home-rigged Steamer. Place one to two inches of water in a skillet. Place a round biscuit cutter in the center of the skillet. Place a heatproof plate on top of the cutter. Top with the food and the skillet's lid.

Coffee Grinder. Once you discover the flavor imparted by toasting and grinding whole spices, you will realize why you need this tool. Keep one coffee grinder specifically for spices. Once a grinder has been used for coffee, it will destroy the flavor of your spices.

Garlic Press. My favorite garlic press is the old-fashioned one-piece metal press (see photo). You can put one or two cloves inside and just push. It's easy to reach in and scrape out the excess pressed garlic. Other presses are harder to clean. Use a press when the garlic needs to be blended evenly throughout a dish.

Grater. I keep three styles of graters on hand. For grating lots of semi-hard cheese, such as cheddar, I like a large box grater with big holes. A flat grater (see photo) is perfect for topping a salad with Parmesan or other hard-grating cheeses. A rotary grater produces long, slender threads of semi-firm cheese such as cheddar.

Knives. Knives are a very personal choice. Choose a brand of knife that feels balanced in your hand and which reportedly holds its edge. Sharpening frequently can shorten the life of some knives. Learn to correctly use a sharpening steel (1) to keep your knives sharp. A basic knife collection should include a chef's knife (2) that feels neither too large nor too small, a paring knife (3) and a serrated bread knife (4). A boning knife (5) and a utility knife (6) are useful as well.

Mandoline. While a food processor can thinly slice most vegetables, I prefer a mandoline for the ability to control the size of the slices. You can purchase the professional (and very expensive) metal variety. The alternative is a plastic model which comes with a set of blades. I use a plastic mandoline all the time and I'm very happy with it. You will delight in the paper-thin slices for cucumber salad and the thin and thicker matchstick pieces for a variety of uses. The smallest blade is a good substitute for a grater. The cut vegetables drop into the attached container and a knife guard protects your fingers.

Microwave. The microwave oven is the great reheating tool. Use the microwave to gently bring refrigerated pasta, grain and vegetable salads to room temperature. A microwave is also the perfect tool for softening cheese, blanching vegetables and even toasting nuts for salads. When performing any of these tasks, be sure to keep an eye on your ingredient and keep the microwave time as short as you can.

Melon Baller. I rarely create melon balls, but I use this tool a lot. It is good for scraping the seeds from a cucumber and removing pear and apple cores without waste. It is also fun to create little cheese balls using goat cheese or a cream cheese mixture, and then roll the balls in chopped nuts or herbs. For this task, lightly spray the inside of the melon baller with olive oil cooking spray.

Mortar and Pestle. I love the mortar and pestle (see photo) for its primal quality. It's so satisfying to hand grind garlic, salt, herbs and spices to be used in salads and dressings. Unlike a coffee grinder, the mortar and pestle allows you to control the texture of the ingredients. Make garlic, herb and chile pastes by pounding in small amounts of liquid such as oil or vinegar.

Salad Spinner. This is perfect for washing, draining and drying a great variety of greens and herbs. For very tender greens, rinse them through a colander and pat dry. I once had a neighbor who washed his greens in an antique colander with a handle. At 6:00 every evening I could see him on his back porch swinging the colander to dry the greens.

Vegetable peeler. A large peeling surface (see photo) is perfect for creating paper-thin matchstick-size pieces, shaving hard cheese and simply peeling vegetables. To create matchstick-size pieces, thickly shave slices of vegetable, such as a carrot or zucchini. Stack the slices, then cut into ⅛- to ¼-inch strips.

Zester. The rasp- or plane-style zester has garnered lots of fans, and with good reason. It's wonderfully sharp, and seems to stay that way. Use a thin-bladed spatula to wipe the zester when gathering the peel, as the edges are very sharp. Use a small hand-held zester (see photo) to create long thin strips of citrus peel.

DRESSING BASICS

Generally speaking, dressings fall into two categories, vinaigrettes and creamy dressings. Vinaigrettes are based on oil and vinegar. Creamy dressings can be based on mayonnaise, sour cream, cream cheese, buttermilk, yogurt or any combination of these.

VINAIGRETTES

The classic combination of oil and vinegar, wine or citrus juice is suitable on almost all delicate greens. Consider the basic mixture as a blank palate upon which you add layers of flavor. Add variation with different kinds of vinegars and oils. Add a little mustard as a thickener. Spice up your dressing or go crazy with herbs!

Vinaigrettes can be shaken or emulsified. Shaken vinaigrettes, as the name implies, are shaken or whisked together just before serving. Added herbs or chopped shallots remain distinct. These dressings are quite pretty, especially with red wine or berry vinegar and floating bits of herbs.

An emulsified vinaigrette is one in which the oil has been gradually blended into vinegar or lemon juice and seasonings. The result is somewhat creamy with the herbs and seasonings visible in tiny flecks. If you'd like the additions (such as herbs, red pepper flakes or sesame seeds) to be visible, stir them into the dressing after the oil has been emulsified into the vinegar.

Well armed with dressing ideas, you will be ready to toss some salads!

ALL ABOUT VINAIGRETTE INGREDIENTS

The simplest dressing is often the best. This is especially true when the highest quality oils and vinegars are used. Perfect greens can be tossed at the table with fragrant olive oil, a sprinkling of sea salt, freshly ground pepper and just a whiff of high quality wine vinegar or balsamic vinegar. The oil is added first to coat the greens, protecting them from the acidity of the vinegar. Salt and pepper then stick to the oiled greens and vinegar brings it all to life.

Vinegar or Citrus Juice. Vinegar can be made from a variety of substances such as red or white wine, sherry, Champagne, cider, berries, herbs and fruit. There are a variety of specialty vinegars available and each contributes its own characteristic. Specialty stores carry herb, garlic and chile-infused vinegars. Stored in a dark, cool spot, these all last for a long time, so it doesn't hurt to stock up. Lemon and lime juice are delicious when they're used instead of vinegar.

Balsamic Vinegar. Because balsamic vinegar is slightly sweet and less acidic than other vinegars, it makes a very pleasant dressing. It is possible to use much less oil in a balsamic-based dressing because there is not as much acid for the oil to cut through. For a fast, fat-free salad, simply sprinkle fresh greens with good quality balsamic vinegar, salt and pepper.

Mustard. Dry or prepared mustard not only adds flavor, but also acts as a thickener and an emulsifier, binding all the other ingredients together. Add mustard to vinaigrette when you're looking for flavor and body.

Salt. Throughout the book, I've specified either kosher (coarse) salt or simply, salt. Kosher (coarse) salt is useful when the dish benefits from little crystals of salt, as on baked pita crisps or fresh tomatoes. In cooking pasta for salads, kosher (coarse) salt takes its time dissolving in the water and seems to season the pasta nicely.

Recipes that call for just "salt," refer to table (mineral) salt or sea salt with a finer grain than kosher (coarse) salt. Either are perfect when dissolving salt in vinegar for a dressing, or to make sure the salt is evenly mixed into a salad. Salts vary in their flavor, so try some mineral salt and sea salt to compare the two. You may even want to try the more expensive specialty sea salts just to see the difference.

Oil. By varying the oil you can transform a dressing's flavor. Vegetable and canola oil have very little flavor, so they're perfect for a neutral base. Olive oil is most widely used for its buttery richness; it sometimes has a peppery flavor. Every olive oil has different characteristics, so try to sample a few before making your purchases. Nut and seed oils add their own character to dressings. Just a teaspoon of nut or seed oil added at the end infuses the dressing with a nutty flavor. Cooking destroys the nuances of these fine oils, so save them for dressing salads and fresh vegetables.

CREAMY DRESSINGS

Many people associate creamy dressings with the store shelf line-up of imitation flavors. But fresh-tasting and healthful creamy dressings can be assembled in a hurry. Creamy dressings are best used on sturdy greens such as romaine and iceberg, and on shredded cabbage, as in coleslaw. The dressing gently coats each lettuce leaf, imparting a wonderful contrast between creamy and crisp. Chopped vegetable salads and sandwich fillings also benefit from creamy dressing.

MAYONNAISE IN CREAMY DRESSINGS

Mayonnaise is the backbone of many creamy dressings. Homemade mayonnaise is lighter in texture and subtler in flavor than the store-bought variety. But because of the rare incidence of salmonella found in unpasteurized eggs, I make homemade mayonnaise from fresh, pasteurized eggs (page 48). I've also successfully used 2 tablespoons of liquid egg substitute in place of each egg. Remember to refrigerate mayonnaise if it will not be used immediately. It will keep, covered and refrigerated, up to one week.

Thicken homemade mayonnaise by gradually blending in additional oil, in very small amounts. Too much oil added too quickly will cause the mixture to become very thin or curdle. You can use this very thick mayonnaise by adding a small amount of lemon juice or warm water.

Although homemade is the best mayonnaise, it's sometimes convenient to have the purchased variety on hand. Use regular, light and low-fat mayonnaise according to your own preference. One tablespoon of extra-virgin olive oil or cream whisked into a cup of purchased mayonnaise improves the flavor considerably.

OTHER INGREDIENTS FOR CREAMY DRESSINGS

To make any creamy dressing, begin with a mayonnaise or other base, then whisk in herbs, spices and flavorings. Since creamy bases are infinitely versatile, your imagination is the limit. Try a little Dijon mustard, a dash of flavored oil, a sprinkling of spices or crumbled saffron. Experiment with Worcestershire sauce, hot pepper sauce or pureed roasted peppers. To allow the flavors to blend, cover and refrigerate your creation for at least an hour before serving. The flavors will intensify, so keep this in mind if you plan to use your dressing the following day.

The following ingredients can be mixed with mayonnaise, with each other, or stand alone as a creamy dressing base. These products range from nonfat and low-fat to rich, full-fat versions. I prefer the low-fat variations for a bit of richness without the gels and emulsifiers that are often found in nonfat dairy products. Like mayonnaise, these dressings always need to be refrigerated.

Buttermilk. Buttermilk adds a wonderful, tangy flavor to dressings. It will need some thickening with mayonnaise or sour cream, or a little of both.

Cream Cheese. This is a terrific dressing thickener. Blend cream cheese with a small amount of cream or milk to make it easy to pour. Stir in fresh herbs and seasonings for a rich dressing or dip.

Sour Cream. This dairy product can form the base of a dressing or it can be mixed with mayonnaise for a lighter texture and a bright, fresh flavor.

Unflavored Yogurt. This is the most tart of the dairy products listed. Unflavored yogurt is delicious blended with thinly sliced cucumbers or stirred into mayonnaise as a dressing base.

CREATE-A-SALAD

Throughout this book, you'll find dressings matched with particular salad recipes. Try the recipes as they're written, or use them as guidelines to create your own combinations. But salads are fun to experiment with too. Use this chart to build a salad by combining different ingredients across each row. Or mix and match ingredients from different rows to branch out on your own salad adventures. Consider combining greens. Toss buttery Boston lettuce with peppery watercress. For color, add anything from bright red radicchio to romaine. Use the chart; use your imagination too!

GREENS	DRESSING	TOPPERS	VEGETABLE/HERBS	FRUIT
Arugula	Walnut oil and red wine vinegar	*Crostini* spread with soft goat cheese, page 35	Diced yellow bell pepper	Dried figs
Boston Lettuce	Vinaigrette with Dijon mustard	Slivered, toasted almonds, page 32	Mixed fresh herbs such as parsley, tarragon and chives	Orange segments
Chinese (Napa) Cabbage	Seasoned rice vinegar	Toasted sesame seeds, page 32	Shredded mint leaves	Tangerine segments
Endive	*Champagne Vinaigrette,* page 43	Prosciutto	Diced jicama	Raspberries
Frisee (curly endive)	*Raspberry Vinaigrette,* page 65	*Sugar-Spiced Walnuts,* page 32 & gorgonzola cheese	Snipped chives	Sliced pears
Iceberg	*Curried Mayonnaise,* page 48	Diced radishes	Sliced celery	Golden raisins
Leaf – Green	*Balsamic Vinaigrette,* page 43	Polenta *Croutons,* page 29	Diced roasted red peppers, page 36	Dried currants
Leaf - Red	*Lemon Buttermilk Dressing,* page 42	Sunflower seeds	Diced radishes	Tart green apples
Radicchio	*Honey Mustard Dressing,* page 86	Diced hard-cooked egg	Baby green beans, blanched	*Preserved Lemons,* slivered, page 38
Romaine	*Ranch-Style Dressing,* page 46	*Sourdough Parmesan Croutons,* page 28	*Roasted Onions,* herbs page 33	Grated orange peel
Spinach	*Poppy Seed Dressing,* page 51	Rye bread *Croutons,* page 29	Minced red onion	Sliced pears
Spring Mix (mesclun)	*Reduced Wine Vinaigrette,* page 49	Pomegranate seeds	Finely shredded green onion	Fuyu persimmon
Watercress	Olive oil and fresh lemon juice	Dry-cured olives	Thinly sliced fennel	Nectarine slices

SALAD BUILDING BLOCKS

A salad is complete simply made from field greens drizzled with fresh lemon juice and fruity olive oil. But then there's the big picture: the variety of salads created by thoughtfully choosing just a few additional ingredients! Offered in this chapter are eight recipes that, when made in advance, allow for quick and creative salads. Take a little time to roast some peppers, make berry vinegar and brown some bread for crisp croutons.

Preserved Lemons, page 38

SOURDOUGH PARMESAN CROUTONS

Cheese-coated croutons are delicious on Romaine with Roasted Onion Dressing *(page 54) and* Iceberg Lettuce Wedges with Roasted Tomato-Thousand Island Dressing *(page 55). Sprinkle these croutons over soups and stews too.*

½ lb. sourdough bread, cut into 1-inch slices
3 tablespoons olive oil
½ cup shredded Parmesan cheese

❶ Heat oven to 400°F. Brush bread slices with olive oil. Cut slices into ½- to 1-inch cubes.

❷ Spread bread cubes over baking sheet. Bake, stirring once or twice, 10 minutes or until golden, but not brown. Transfer to large bowl.

❸ While croutons are hot, add Parmesan cheese; toss to coat well. Let cool until crisp.

❹ When cool, store in airtight container. Croutons will stay fresh in sealed plastic bag or container 1 week or longer.

6 cups.

Preparation time: 8 minutes. Ready to serve: 18 minutes.

Per serving: 100 calories, 5 g total fat (1.5 g saturated fat), 5 mg cholesterol, 185 mg sodium, 0.5 g fiber.

CROUTONS

Quick to make and long-lasting to store, homemade Croutons are fresher, less expensive and lower in fat than most purchased Croutons. For variety, make them plain or seasoned with garlic powder, salt or spice mixes.

½ lb. sliced bread
3 tablespoons olive oil
1 tablespoon salt or seasoning mix, if desired

1 Heat oven to 400°F. Brush bread slices with olive oil. Cut slices into ½- to 1-inch cubes.

2 Spread bread cubes over baking sheet. Bake, stirring once or twice, 10 minutes or until golden, but not brown. Transfer to large bowl.

3 While croutons are hot, if desired, sprinkle with salt or seasoning mix; toss to coat. Let cool until crisp.

4 When cool, store in airtight container. Croutons will stay fresh in sealed plastic bag or container 1 week or longer.

6 cups.
Preparation time: 8 minutes. Ready to serve: 18 minutes.

Per serving: 80 calories, 4 g total fat (0.5 g saturated fat), 0 mg cholesterol, 685 mg sodium, 0.5 g fiber.

CHEF'S NOTE
- Use leftovers to their fullest. Make Croutons from day-old dark rye bread, corn bread and leftover sliced polenta.

RASPBERRY VINEGAR

Vinegar simmered with fresh berries and strained will keep for months. This gem-colored vinegar creates beautiful vinaigrettes with a multitude of uses.

2   cups (12 oz.) fresh raspberries
2   cups white vinegar

❶ Wash raspberries; drain. Pat berries dry with paper towel.

❷ In nonreactive saucepan, combine raspberries and vinegar. Heat over medium heat until almost simmering.

❸ Let cool to room temperature. Pour into clean jar with lid. Cover; let stand in cool, dark place 7 to 10 days.

❹ Pour through sieve to strain berries. Do not press berries; rather, let sieve sit with berries over a bowl to gradually collect juices. Using funnel, pour into clean bottle.

❺ If desired, garnish with bay leaf or herb of choice.

2 cups.

Preparation time: 5 minutes. Ready to use: 7 days.

Per serving: 1 calorie, 0 g total fat (0 g saturated fat), 0 mg cholesterol, 0 mg sodium, 0 g fiber.

VARIATION   More Berries

Use the same proportions of berries to vinegar for strawberries, blackberries or any other soft berries.

SUGAR-SPICED WALNUTS

Sweet, peppery and crunchy all at once, Sugar-Spiced Walnuts *instantly add magic to a salad.*

¼ cup sugar
½ teaspoon freshly ground pepper
¼ teaspoon cayenne pepper
¼ teaspoon ground ginger
¼ teaspoon salt
1 cup walnut halves

❶ In small bowl, combine sugar, ground pepper, cayenne, ginger and salt; set aside.

❷ Heat heavy skillet over medium-high heat. Add walnuts in a single layer. Cook, stirring frequently, about 3 minutes or until fragrant and lightly browned. Stir in sugar mixture.

❸ Cook, stirring constantly, until walnuts are well coated with sugar mixture, about 1 minute. Do not let sugar dissolve completely; leave some grainy texture on the walnuts. Transfer to plate; let cool.

> **CHEF'S NOTE**
> • Other nuts — such as pecans, almonds and cashews — may be used. Try using other spices such as cumin and cardamom.

❹ For easy cleanup, immediately place hot skillet under warm water.

1 cup.

Preparation time: 8 minutes. Ready to serve: 12 minutes.

Per serving: 105 calories, 7.5 g total fat (0.5 g saturated fat), 0 mg cholesterol, 75 mg sodium, 0.5 g fiber.

TOASTED NUTS AND CEREAL

Toasted nuts and cereal add crunch to salads of almost any style, not to mention loads of flavor. Toast mixed nuts and cereal, and keep them on hand in a sealed container for a week or longer. Here are three methods for toasting nuts and cereal.

Oven Method. Heat oven to 400°F. Spread nuts or cereal in a single layer on baking sheet. Bake 8 to 10 minutes or until fragrant but not dark. Stir once or twice during baking. If desired, sprinkle with salt while warm. Let cool before using.

Stovetop Method. Heat heavy skillet over medium-high heat. Add nuts in a single layer. Cook, stirring frequently, about 3 minutes or until fragrant but not dark. If desired, sprinkle with salt while warm. Let cool before using.

Microwave Method. Place up to 1 cup nuts in a single layer on microwave-safe plate. Microwave on High 3 to 4 minutes or until fragrant. Stir once or twice during cooking. If desired, sprinkle with salt while warm. Let cool before using.

ROASTED ONIONS AND GARLIC

Roasted Onions and Garlic *are useful in so many salads in so many ways. They can be pureed and used in a dressing, as in* Sweet Potato Salad *(page 159). They can be diced and roasted to be tossed with vegetables, as in* Succotash Salad *(page 76). Pasta, beans, grains and greens all become a little sweeter with roasted onions.*

1 tablespoon olive oil
2 onions, cut into 1-inch pieces, or cut from top to stem end into thin wedges
6 garlic cloves, peeled, halved

❶ Heat oven to 375°F. Brush baking sheet with olive oil. Spread onions and garlic over prepared baking sheet; stir to lightly coat with oil.

❷ Bake, stirring once, 20 minutes or until tender and lightly browned.

2½ cups.

Preparation time: 5 minutes. Ready to serve: 25 minutes.

Per serving: 20 calories, 1.5 g total fat (0 g saturated fat), 0 mg cholesterol, 1 mg sodium, 0.5 g fiber.

ROSTINI

Crisp "little toasts" are embellished croutons to serve alongside a salad. The tomato is optional, but adds nice flavor and a bit of color. For more substantial Crostini, *top with a bit of prepared pesto or tapenade.*

1 lb. baguette, cut into thin diagonal strips
2 tablespoons olive oil
1 garlic clove, halved lengthwise
1 plum tomato, halved crosswise
⅛ teaspoon salt

❶ Heat grill or broiler. Lightly brush both sides of baguette slices with olive oil. Cook baguette slices 4 to 6 inches from heat, on one side until golden, about 3 minutes. Remove from heat; let cool. (Slices will crisp slightly as they cool.)

❷ Rub one side of each slice with cut side of garlic and cut end of tomato. Rub hard for maximum flavor. Sprinkle with salt.

4 servings.

Preparation time: 12 minutes. Ready to serve: 15 minutes.

Per serving: 370 calories, 10.5 g total fat (2 g saturated fat), 0 mg cholesterol, 735 mg sodium, 3.5 g fiber.

ROASTED PEPPERS

Roasted Peppers are easy to prepare and real time-savers to have on hand. They brighten up a last-minute salad and look beautiful on a platter with olives, cheese and crackers. Completely submerged in olive oil and refrigerated, they keep a month or longer.

2   red, green or yellow bell peppers, or a combination of colors
    Extra-virgin olive oil (if not using peppers right away)

❶ Heat grill or broiler. Cook peppers 4 to 6 inches from heat, 8 to 10 minutes, turning occasionally, until charred on all sides.

❷ Place peppers in resealable plastic bag to steam; let stand 5 minutes. Using paring knife and fingers, remove skin. Do not rinse under water. Cut peppers into large pieces; discard seeds and membrane.

❸ Peppers are now ready to use. If storing peppers, cut into large pieces. Place in resealable jar. Add olive oil to completely cover peppers. Cover jar; refrigerate until ready to use.

1½ cups.

Preparation time: 5 minutes. Ready to use: 15 minutes.

Per serving: 5 calories, 0 g total fat (0 g saturated fat), 0 mg cholesterol, 0.5 mg sodium, 0 g fiber.

CHEF'S NOTE
• If storing peppers, they must always be submerged in oil and refrigerated.

ROASTING FOR EXTRAORDINARY FLAVOR

Roasted peppers, onions, garlic and other vegetables appear throughout this book. While it may seem a time-consuming extra step, roasting results in extraordinary flavor.

Many foods contain sugar in the form of carbohydrates. When these foods are roasted or grilled, the high heat caramelizes these sugars, enhancing the flavor. At first the high heat brings out sweetness. As the food continues to roast or grill, this sweetness develops into rich, complex flavors. All of this happens just by brushing the vegetables with a little bit of oil and roasting them.

Roasting Methods

Oven Roasting. See *Roasted Onions and Garlic* (page 33). Small cuts of vegetables will take less time; larger cuts or whole vegetables may take longer, but will develop more flavor.

• Heat oven to 375°F. Drizzle vegetables with a small amount of olive oil. Rub or toss to lightly coat with oil.

• Bake 15 to 20 minutes or until skins are brown but not blackened. Remove from oven; let cool.

• For roasted peppers, use your fingers or a sharp paring knife to pull off skins.

Pan or Skillet Roasting. Mexican and other cuisines regularly pan-roast tomatoes, garlic, onions, seeds and peppers in a dry, cast-iron skillet or a flat Spanish griddle (*comal*) over medium-high heat. This gives extra flavor depth to the finished dish.

• Heat a heavy skillet (cast iron works best) over medium heat.

• Arrange vegetable slices or cubes in skillet with space between each piece. Cook, turning to brown all sides, until slightly soft and browned but not blackened.

• Tomato slices will take about 3 minutes. Whole garlic cloves and pieces of pepper and onion will take 8 to 10 minutes.

• Seeds will take just 1 to 2 minutes, stirring frequently.

Broiling or Grilling. This is a favorite method for roasting peppers. The skins get blistered and dark, and should be removed before proceeding with the recipe.

• Heat broiler or grill. Place peppers on rack in pan under broiler or directly over grill flame. Broil or grill 8 to 10 minutes, turning occasionally, until charred on all sides.

• Place in resealable plastic bag to steam; let sit 5 minutes. Using a paring knife and fingers, remove skin. Do not rinse under water. Cut peppers into large pieces, discard seeds and membrane.

• If storing peppers, cut into large pieces. Place in resealable jar. Add olive oil to completely cover. Cover jar and refrigerate until ready to use.

PRESERVED LEMONS

Fresh, plump lemons — covered in kosher (coarse) salt and allowed to ripen — become sweet and salty. Eureka lemons, those usually seen in supermarkets, are good for this use because of their thick skin. The thinner-skinned and sweeter Meyer lemon yields a more tender preserved lemon, although with slightly less peel.

9   lemons (Meyer lemons, if available), washed in warm water
½   cup kosher (coarse) salt
2   cinnamon sticks
½   cup fresh lemon juice

❶ Cut lemons into quarters lengthwise from the top to within about ½ inch of stem end. (Do not separate quarters.)

❷ Place salt in small bowl. Holding 1 lemon over bowl, cover insides with salt.

❸ Place 1 tablespoon of the salt in bottom of large jar. Pack cut lemons and cinnamon sticks tightly into jar, sprinkling remaining salt between each layer. Add lemon juice, leaving some air space. Close jar tightly.

❹ Leave jar in warm place about 3 weeks or until peel is soft. Occasionally turn jar over and back to cover lemons with salt and juice.

❺ To use, rinse salt from lemons and separate pulp from peel. Both pulp and peel can be used.

9 lemons.

Preparation time: 15 minutes. Ready to serve: 3 weeks.

Per serving: 5 calories, 0 g total fat (0 g saturated fat), 0 mg cholesterol, 260 mg sodium, 0 g fiber.

CHEF'S NOTE

• The peel is the most frequently used part of a preserved lemon. Sliced thinly, it can be an ingredient or garnish for a variety of green, pasta, grain and rice salads. Left in larger pieces, Preserved Lemons are delicious in meat and vegetable braises. The pulp can also be sparingly blended into vinaigrettes.

SALAD DRESSINGS

Salads wouldn't be salads without their dressings. Dressings can be drizzled, dolloped or tossed depending on the salad's style and texture. Sometimes dressings aren't obvious, as in pasta and grain salads, when the dressing is an integral part of the dish. Throughout this book, salads have dressings built into each recipe. But feel free to mix and match dressings and ingredients. Use the dressings in this chapter and the Create-A-Salad chart on page 25 for inspiration in creating your own signature salads from scratch.

Poppy Seed Dressing, page 51

BUTTERMILK DRESSING

This is another blank sheet of paper upon which you can create any number of flavors. If you're looking for a low-fat creamy dressing — this can be it. Use the low-fat versions of each of the ingredients. Avoid the nonfat ingredients, because they often contain gels and emulsifiers which detract from the fresh flavor. I have, however, seen exceptions to this. It pays to read labels.

¼   cup buttermilk
¼   cup sour cream
¼   cup prepared *Mayonnaise* (page 48)

❶ In small bowl, combine buttermilk, sour cream and Mayonnaise. Whisk to blend well.

❷ Cover and refrigerate 30 minutes to allow dressing to thicken.

¾ cup.

Preparation time: 5 minutes. Ready to use: 30 minutes.

Per serving: 80 calories, 8.5 g total fat (2 g saturated fat), 15 mg cholesterol, 40 mg sodium, 0 g fiber.

VARIATION   Lemon Buttermilk Dressing
Stir 2 teaspoons grated lemon peel into ¾ cup *Buttermilk Dressing*.

ASIC VINAIGRETTE

This is a dressing to experiment with. Try it with or without mustard, and with different combinations of oil and vinegar or fruit juice.

- 2 tablespoons vinegar
- 1 tablespoon minced shallot
- ½ teaspoon Dijon mustard (optional)
- ¼ teaspoon salt
- ⅛ teaspoon freshly ground pepper
- ¼ cup oil

❶ In small bowl or blender, combine vinegar, shallot, mustard, salt and pepper. Slowly whisk or blend in oil.

❷ If not using right away, transfer dressing to a jar with a lid; cover. Shake, just before adding to salad.

⅓ cup.

Preparation time: 5 minutes. Ready to serve: 5 minutes.

Per serving: 120 calories, 13.5 g total fat (2 g saturated fat), 0 mg cholesterol, 155 mg sodium, 0 g fiber.

VARIATION Balsamic Vinaigrette

Substitute 2 tablespoons wine vinegar for the vinegar. Substitute extra-virgin olive oil for the oil.

VARIATION Champagne Vinaigrette

Substitute 2 tablespoons Champagne vinegar for the vinegar. Substitute extra-virgin or hazelnut oil for the oil.

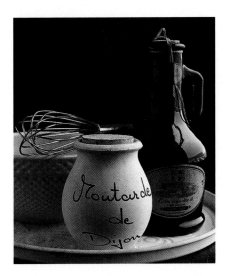

HERB VINAIGRETTE

For a blended herb dressing, combine fresh herbs in the blender with the vinegar mixture. For "floating" herbs, finely chop or tear the herbs and stir them in at the end.

2 tablespoons chopped fresh basil or 1 tablespoon chopped fresh oregano
2 tablespoons white wine vinegar
1 tablespoon chopped shallot
¼ teaspoon salt
⅛ teaspoon freshly ground pepper
¼ cup extra-virgin olive oil

❶ In blender, combine basil, vinegar, shallot, salt and pepper. Cover and blend until smooth. With blender running, gradually blend in olive oil.

½ cup.

Preparation time: 5 minutes. Ready to serve: 5 minutes.

Per serving: 120 calories, 13.5 g total fat (2 g saturated fat), 0 mg cholesterol, 145 mg sodium, 0 g fiber.

RANCH-STYLE DRESSING

Buttermilk and Mayonnaise (page 48) form the base of this popular creamy dressing. Stir in herbs, a dash of cayenne pepper, a little Worcestershire sauce, or any seasoning that will give the dressing, and your salad, a lift.

½ cup buttermilk
½ cup prepared *Mayonnaise* (page 48)
2 tablespoons chopped chives
1 garlic clove, minced
½ teaspoon salt
¼ teaspoon freshly ground pepper

1 In small bowl, combine buttermilk, Mayonnaise, chives, garlic, salt and pepper. Cover and refrigerate 30 minutes to allow flavors to blend.

¼ cup.

Preparation time: 5 minutes. Ready to serve: 35 minutes.

Per serving: 90 calories, 9.5 g total fat (1.5 g saturated fat), 15 mg cholesterol, 200 mg sodium, 0 g fiber.

AYONNAISE

In any of the upcoming recipes calling for Mayonnaise, *feel free to use any of the purchased varieties. Regular, light and low-fat work equally well. But you can make your own great Mayonnaise too. Here's how:*

1	pasteurized egg or 2 tablespoons liquid egg substitute
2	teaspoons fresh lemon juice
1	teaspoon Dijon mustard
¼	teaspoon salt
⅛	teaspoon freshly ground pepper
⅔	cup extra-virgin olive oil or vegetable oil

❶ In blender, combine egg or egg substitute, lemon juice, mustard, salt, pepper and ¼ cup oil. Process until smooth, about 10 seconds.

❷ With blender running, slowly drizzle in the remaining oil until mixture has thickened.

❸ Taste and adjust salt, if necessary.

About 1 cup.

Preparation time: 8 minutes. Ready to serve: 8 minutes.

Per serving: 170 calories, 18.5 g total fat (2.5 g saturated fat), 26.5 mg cholesterol, 90 mg sodium, 0 g fiber.

VARIATION Blue Cheese Dressing

Choose a mild blue cheese for a delicate salad. Choose a stronger blue cheese for a salad with more bold ingredients. To one recipe of *Mayonnaise* (about 1 cup), add ¼ to ½ cup of crumbled blue cheese and 3 tablespoons of cream or milk.

VARIATION Curried Mayonnaise

If you're a curry lover, you'll know that this is a flavor that pairs with a wide variety of foods. Curried Mayonnaise is delicious on everything from turkey salad (see page 125) to fresh fruit. In small skillet over medium heat, toast 1 teaspoon to 1 tablespoon curry powder until fragrant. Let cool. Stir into 1 cup of Mayonnaise.

REDUCED WINE VINAIGRETTE

Using reduced wine in place of vinegar makes a flavorful dressing that is less acidic than traditional vinaigrettes. With this dressing, you can create a salad that pairs nicely with dry white wine.

½   cup Chardonnay
 2   tablespoons minced shallots
¼   teaspoon salt
¼   teaspoon freshly ground pepper
¼   cup extra-virgin olive oil

❶ In small saucepan, combine wine and shallots. Bring to a simmer over medium heat. Simmer until wine is reduced to ¼ cup, about 10 minutes.

❷ Stir in salt and pepper until salt has dissolved. Let cool slightly. Whisk in olive oil.

½ cup.

Preparation time: 5 minutes. Ready to serve: 15 minutes.

Per serving: 125 calories, 13.5 g total fat (2 g saturated fat), 0 mg cholesterol, 150 mg sodium, 0 g fiber.

POPPY SEED DRESSING

Slightly sweet and slightly sour flavors, combined with poppy seeds, make a versatile combination. It's equally delicious on greens, vegetables and fruit. Poppy seeds also make an appearance in the mango and ginger dressing for Tropical Fruit Salad *(page 142)*

2   tablespoons cider vinegar
1   tablespoon poppy seeds
1   tablespoon sweet hot mustard
1   tablespoon honey
¼   teaspoon salt
⅛   teaspoon freshly ground pepper
⅓   cup vegetable oil

❶ In small bowl, combine vinegar, poppy seeds, mustard, honey, salt and pepper. Whisk in oil. Or, for a creamier dressing, combine all ingredients in blender; beat until smooth.

⅔ cup.
Preparation time: 5 minutes. Ready to serve: 5 minutes.

Per serving: 130 calories, 12.5 g total fat (2 g saturated fat), 0 mg cholesterol, 120 mg sodium, 0.5 g fiber.

GREEN SALADS

When most of us think salad, a green salad comes to mind. Even so, green salads are amazingly versatile. Dress them heartily with rich, creamy dressings and substantial toppings. Make them sleek with light vinaigrettes and pretty herbs. Spike them with the peppery bite of arugula. Mellow them with the silky texture of butter lettuce. Sweeten them with dried cherries. Make them tart with lime and salt. Keep them seasonal and they'll always be fresh.

Frisee with Hazelnuts and
Three Artisan Cheeses, page 65

ROMAINE WITH ROASTED ONION DRESSING

Reminiscent of Caesar salad, this party-size salad tastes like sweet, roasted onions. With the dressing and croutons lasting up to a week when properly stored, the ingredients are handy for a last-minute salad any time.

ROASTED ONION DRESSING
1 tablespoon olive oil
2 cups coarsely chopped Vidalia, Maui or other sweet onion
2 garlic cloves, halved
2 tablespoons water
2 tablespoons extra-virgin olive oil
2 tablespoons fresh lemon juice
1 tablespoon freshly grated lemon peel
2 teaspoons Worcestershire sauce
1 teaspoon salt
½ teaspoon freshly ground pepper

SALAD
1 large or 2 small heads romaine lettuce
2 cups prepared *Sourdough Parmesan Croutons* (page 28)

❶ Heat oven to 375°F. Brush baking sheet with 1 tablespoon olive oil. Top with onion and garlic; stir to lightly coat with oil. Bake 20 minutes or until tender.

❷ In blender, combine onion mixture, water, extra-virgin olive oil, lemon juice, lemon peel, Worcestershire sauce, salt and pepper. Cover; blend until smooth.

❸ Cut lettuce just above core; place in large bowl of ice water. Soak 5 minutes; drain well. Cut lettuce head crosswise into 1½-inch pieces. Toss with dressing. Divide among 8 serving plates. Sprinkle Croutons over each serving.

8 (1-cup) servings.

Preparation time: 15 minutes. Ready to serve: 35 minutes.

Per serving: 125 calories, 8 g total fat (1.5 g saturated fat), 1 mg cholesterol, 405 mg sodium, 2.5 g fiber.

ICEBERG LETTUCE WEDGES WITH ROASTED TOMATO-THOUSAND ISLAND DRESSING

This is a fancy version of iceberg lettuce with Thousand Island dressing. Coring and soaking head lettuce keeps the lettuce crisp for days.

¾ cup prepared *Mayonnaise* (page 48)

½ teaspoon hot pepper sauce

2 tablespoons grated green bell pepper

2 tablespoons grated onion

4 plum tomatoes, thickly sliced

1 head iceberg lettuce

❶ In small bowl, mix Mayonnaise and hot pepper sauce. Stir in bell pepper and onion. Cover and refrigerate.

❷ Heat large nonstick skillet until hot. Arrange tomato slices in skillet in a single layer. Cook until slightly charred on 1 side, about 5 minutes. Do not allow tomatoes to soften. Remove to platter, charred-side up.

❸ Cut one-fourth of the roasted tomato slices into ¼-inch pieces. Stir tomato pieces into Mayonnaise mixture; cover and refrigerate.

❹ Remove lettuce core. Cut lettuce head in half from core-end to top. Cut each half into 2 wedges. Place 1 wedge on each serving plate. Surround with charred tomato slices. Drizzle dressing over lettuce wedges. Serve remaining dressing on the side.

4 servings.

Preparation time: 15 minutes. Ready to serve: 18 minutes.

Per serving: 285 calories, 28.5 g total fat (4 g saturated fat), 40 mg cholesterol, 155 mg sodium, 2.5 g fiber.

SPINACH SALAD WITH HONEY BELL TANGERINES

Honey bell tangerines are larger and contain more juice than the more common honey variety. If honey bells aren't available, use 4 or 5 honey tangerines.

TANGERINE VINAIGRETTE

- 3 honey bell tangerines
- 1 tablespoon chopped fresh Italian parsley
- 1 tablespoon minced shallot
- 1 tablespoon red wine vinegar
- 1 teaspoon Dijon mustard
- ½ teaspoon salt
- ¼ teaspoon freshly ground pepper
- ⅓ cup extra-virgin olive oil

SALAD

- 6 cups baby spinach leaves
- ½ small red onion, cut into thin wedges
- ¾ cup prepared *Sugar-Spiced Walnuts* (page 32)
- ½ cup (2 oz.) crumbled feta cheese

❶ Using sharp knife, peel tangerines, cutting away all white pulp and thin outer membrane. Holding over a bowl to catch juice, cut between inner membranes to remove segments. Reserve segments.

❷ In medium bowl, combine ¼ cup tangerine juice, parsley, shallot, vinegar, mustard, salt and pepper; blend with wire whisk. While whisking, slowly drizzle in olive oil.

❸ In large bowl just before serving, toss spinach, onion and reserved tangerine segments. Add dressing; toss again. Sprinkle Sugar-Spiced Walnuts and feta over each serving.

6 (1-cup) servings.

Preparation time: 20 minutes. Ready to serve: 20 minutes.

Per serving: 290 calories, 22.5 g total fat (4 g saturated fat), 10 mg cholesterol, 465 mg sodium, 4 g fiber.

$\mathcal{W}$ATERCRESS SALAD WITH CURRIED RICE VINEGAR

Seasoned rice vinegar is a dieter's delight. This light, not-too-pungent vinegar can be used without oil, or with just a little oil as in this curry dressing for watercress.

CURRIED RICE VINAIGRETTE
1 teaspoon curry powder
1 garlic clove
2 teaspoons grated fresh ginger
½ teaspoon salt
¼ cup seasoned rice vinegar
½ teaspoon sugar
2 tablespoons peanut oil or vegetable oil
1 teaspoon sesame oil

SALAD
2 bunches watercress
¼ red onion, thinly sliced
½ carrot, peeled, cut into matchstick-size strips (¼x¼x1-inch)
½ cucumber, peeled, cut into matchstick-size strips (¼x¼x1-inch)

❶ In small skillet, toast curry powder over medium heat until fragrant.

❷ Using mortar and pestle or side of chef's knife, mash garlic, ginger and salt into a paste; transfer to small bowl. Add curry powder, vinegar and sugar; stir until well blended. Whisk in peanut and sesame oils.

❸ In large bowl, toss watercress and onion with just enough of the dressing to coat. Sprinkle with carrot and cucumber.

6 (1-cup) servings.

Preparation time: 20 minutes. Ready to serve: 20 minutes.

Per serving: 60 calories, 5.5 g total fat (1 g saturated fat), 0 mg cholesterol, 205 mg sodium, 1 g fiber.

CHEF'S NOTE
• When made in the blender, this dressing becomes a creamy curry dressing that is wonderful dolloped on fresh melon and pineapple.

$\mathcal{M}$IXED GREENS WITH CREAMY CUCUMBER DRESSING

Pre-washed mixed greens make salad-making a snap! This dressing is light in flavor and enhances delicate lettuces. Sweet 100s are very tiny cherry tomatoes that pack big flavor; if you can't find them, cut regular cherry tomatoes into quarters.

CREAMY CUCUMBER DRESSING
- ¼ cup buttermilk
- ¼ cup sour cream
- ¼ cup prepared *Mayonnaise* (page 48)
- ½ cucumber, peeled, seeded and chopped*
- 2 tablespoons chopped onion
- ½ teaspoon salt
- ¼ teaspoon ground white pepper
- ¼ teaspoon ground cumin
- 1 tablespoon finely chopped fresh Italian parsley

SALAD
- 8 cups (10 oz.) mixed spring greens
- 1 cup Sweet 100 cherry tomatoes
- 6 seeded crackers, broken into large pieces

❶ In blender, combine buttermilk, sour cream, Mayonnaise, cucumber, onion, salt, pepper and cumin. Cover; blend until smooth. Stir in parsley.

❷ In large bowl, toss greens and tomatoes. Add just enough dressing to coat greens; toss. Divide salad among 6 plates. Top each with cracker pieces.

6 (1-cup) servings.

Preparation time: 15 minutes. Ready to serve: 15 minutes.

Per serving: 125 calories, 9 g total fat (2 g saturated fat), 15 mg cholesterol, 280 mg sodium, 2.5 g fiber.

TIP *To remove cucumber seeds, peel and cut cucumber into halves lengthwise. Use a grapefruit spoon or melon baller to scrape away the seeds.

GRILLED RADICCHIO WITH SHAVED PARMESAN

Grilled Radicchio with Shaved Parmesan *is a perfect accompaniment to a barbecued meal. Heat the oil and garlic in advance. The radicchio takes just a short time to cook and can be grilled while the entrée is being served.*

 2 heads radicchio
 10 garlic cloves, halved
 ¼ cup (2 oz.) diced lean bacon
 ½ cup olive oil
 3 tablespoons balsamic vinegar
 ¼ teaspoon salt
 ¼ teaspoon freshly ground pepper
 2 oz. Sonoma Dry Jack or Parmesan cheese, sliced with vegetable peeler

❶ Heat grill.

❷ Cut core from radicchio. Place in bowl of ice water; let soak 5 minutes. Remove and drain well.

❸ In small saucepan, combine garlic, bacon and olive oil. Heat slowly over low heat until bacon is cooked and garlic is soft, about 15 minutes.

❹ Brush radicchio with garlic-pancetta oil. Transfer to grill. Cook radicchio 4 to 6 inches from heat, turning occasionally, until radicchio is softened but not charred, about 5 minutes.

❺ Place 2 wedges grilled radicchio on each of 4 salad plates. Drizzle each serving with 1 heaping tablespoon warm garlic-pancetta oil. Drizzle generously with balsamic vinegar; sprinkle with salt and pepper. Top with a few shavings of cheese.

4 servings.

Preparation time: 15 minutes. Ready to serve: 35 minutes.

Per serving: 420 calories, 40.5 g total fat (10 g saturated fat), 20 mg cholesterol, 490 mg sodium, 1.5 g fiber.

RED AND WHITE ENDIVE SLAW WITH WALNUTS AND APPLES

It's not just Belgian anymore! Thanks to a California innovator, beautiful endive is now produced in our own country. This is a great salad for entertaining because it can be tossed and refrigerated for 2 or 3 hours, then arranged just before serving.

LEMON AND HONEY DRESSING
- 2 teaspoons freshly grated lemon peel
- 3 tablespoons fresh lemon juice
- 2 teaspoons honey
- ¼ teaspoon salt
- ⅛ teaspoon ground white pepper
- 2 tablespoons extra-virgin olive oil

SALAD
- 2 red endives or 1 head radicchio
- 2 white endives
- ½ bulb fennel, white part only, cut into matchstick-size strips (¼x¼x1-inch)
- 1 crisp apple, such as Gala or Granny Smith, cut into matchstick-size strips (¼x¼x1-inch)
- ½ cup toasted walnuts
- ½ cup (2 oz.) crumbled Gorgonzola cheese

❶ In small bowl, combine lemon peel, lemon juice, honey, salt and pepper. Whisk in olive oil.

❷ Reserve 8 whole red endive leaves and 8 white leaves. Gently rinse, dry and wrap in paper towel; refrigerate until serving. Gently rinse and dry remaining endive leaves; cut crosswise into thin slivers.

❸ In large bowl, combine slivered endive leaves, fennel, apple and walnuts. Toss with dressing. Arrange 2 red and 2 white endive leaves on each of 4 salad plates. Place about ½ cup slivered endive mixture in center of each plate. Sprinkle each serving with Gorgonzola.

4 servings.

Preparation time: 20 minutes. Ready to serve: 20 minutes.

Per serving: 250 calories, 19.5 g total fat (5 g saturated fat), 12.5 mg cholesterol, 405 mg sodium, 4 g fiber.

SPRING GREENS WITH SWEET-AND-SOUR APRICOT DRESSING

Celebrate spring with the arrival of fresh apricots. Arrange them around the salad to enhance the apricot dressing. This is a no-oil dressing, making for a fat-free salad.

SWEET-AND-SOUR APRICOT DRESSING
- ¼ cup apricot jam
- 2 tablespoons white wine vinegar
- 1 tablespoon minced shallot
- ¼ teaspoon crushed red pepper
- ¼ teaspoon salt

SALAD
- 6 cups (8 oz.) mixed spring greens
- ½ cucumber, peeled, cut into matchstick-size strips (¼x¼x1-inch)
- 2 yellow pattypan squash or 1 yellow summer squash, cut into matchstick-size strips (¼x¼x1-inch)
- 1 cup alfalfa sprouts, washed well, drained and patted dry with paper towels
- 1 cup prepared rye bread *Croutons* (page 29)

GARNISH
- 6 ripe apricots, each cut into 6 wedges, if available

❶ In small saucepan, combine jam, vinegar, shallot, crushed red pepper and salt. Heat over medium-high heat, stirring occasionally, until jam has melted. Let cool.

❷ In large bowl, combine greens, cucumber, squash and sprouts. Just before serving, drizzle dressing over salad; toss well. Sprinkle with Croutons. Garnish with fresh apricot wedges.

6 (1-cup) servings.

Preparation time: 15 minutes. Ready to serve: 20 minutes.

Per serving: 95 calories, 2 g total fat (0 g saturated fat), 0 mg cholesterol, 360 mg sodium, 3.5 g fiber.

FRISEE WITH HAZELNUTS AND THREE ARTISAN CHEESES

Preciously priced frisee (curly endive) is worth serving once in a while for its beauty, texture and fabulous flavor. This salad pulls out all the stops —
Raspberry Vinegar (page 30), *hazelnuts and your choice of artisan cheeses.*

RASPBERRY VINAIGRETTE
2 tablespoons prepared *Raspberry Vinegar* (page 30)
1 tablespoon minced shallot
¼ teaspoon sugar
¼ teaspoon salt
⅛ teaspoon ground white pepper
¼ cup extra-virgin olive oil
2 tablespoons hazelnut oil

SALAD
1 large head frisee (curly endive)
½ cup toasted chopped hazelnuts
4 oz. each Three Artisan Cheeses (see Chef's Note)

GARNISH
½ pint fresh raspberries

❶ In small bowl, combine Raspberry Vinegar, shallot, sugar, salt and pepper. Whisk in olive and hazelnut oils.

❷ Separate frisee leaves; wash well and pat dry. In large bowl, combine frisee and dressing; toss gently to mix. Arrange on 8 salad plates.

❸ Sprinkle each salad with hazelnuts. Crumble or slice some of each cheese. Arrange a little of each cheese on each salad. Arrange a few raspberries around edge of each plate.

8 (1-cup) servings.

Preparation time: 20 minutes. Ready to serve: 20 minutes.

Per serving: 310 calories, 27.5 g total fat (9.5 g saturated fat), 35 mg cholesterol, 455 mg sodium, 3.5 g fiber.

CHEF'S NOTE
• There is a now a bewildering array of good domestic and foreign cheeses made by producers of artisan cheese. Choose three very different styles — such as a creamy Brie, a crumbly, rich blue and a harder slicing goat or sheep's milk cheese.

VEGETABLE SALADS

Vegetable salads are capable of many tasks. They can take the place of green salads, either before or after an entrée. Some, like Caprese, can be enjoyed as summer luncheons on their own. Chilled vegetables with a drizzle of dressing make delicious side dishes in warm weather. Always plan your menu carefully so the salad course is easy to serve.

Caprese, page 78

67

GRILLED SQUASH AND TOMATO SALAD WITH HERBS

Take full advantage of outdoor cooking by including grilled vegetables on your menu. A grill basket makes easy work of turning the vegetables. During winter months, a ridged grill pan used on the stovetop works very well.

SPICE-INFUSED OIL
- 2 teaspoons cardamom seeds
- 2 teaspoons cumin seeds
- 2 teaspoons fennel seeds
- 1 teaspoon crushed red pepper
- ¾ cup olive oil
- 3 garlic cloves, finely chopped

GRILLED VEGETABLES
- 1 yellow summer squash, ends trimmed, cut lengthwise into ¼-inch-thick slices
- 1 zucchini, ends trimmed, cut lengthwise into ¼-inch-thick slices
- 1 Japanese eggplant, ends trimmed, cut lengthwise into ¼-inch-thick slices
- 1 red onion, cut into ½-inch slices
- 1 beefsteak tomato, cut into ½-inch slices
- 3 tablespoons balsamic or red wine vinegar
- 3 tablespoons chopped fresh oregano or basil
- ½ teaspoon salt
- ½ teaspoon freshly ground pepper
- 1 cup (4 oz.) crumbled goat cheese or sheep cheese

❶ In small skillet, toast cardamom seeds, cumin seeds, fennel seeds and crushed red pepper over medium heat until fragrant; let cool. Grind spices using mortar and pestle or coffee grinder reserved for spices.

❷ In small saucepan, warm olive oil, garlic and toasted spices over low heat 15 minutes or until oil is fragrant. Let cool. Infused oil may be prepared several hours before using.

❸ Heat grill. Brush summer squash, zucchini, eggplant, onion and tomato with some of the infused oil. Place vegetables in grill basket or on lightly oiled ridged grill pan. Cook 4 to 6 inches from heat, turning frequently, until tender but not too soft. Onion will take about 5 minutes; eggplant, zucchini and tomato about 3 minutes. Layer grilled vegetables on large platter, sprinkling vinegar, oregano, salt and pepper on each layer. Sprinkle with goat cheese.

6 servings.

Preparation time: 30 minutes. Ready to serve: 45 minutes.

Per serving: 205 calories, 18 g total fat (4.5 g saturated fat), 15 mg cholesterol, 265 mg sodium, 2.5 g fiber.

CHEF'S NOTE
- An earthy, flavorful cheese, such as a slightly aged Spanish goat cheese, really adds to the vegetable flavor.

CELERY ROOT SALAD ON ARUGULA

Celery Root Salad on Arugula is a delightful and crunchy winter salad. Avoid purchasing a giant celery root. Instead, choose one that is smaller and free of blemishes. Celery root, also called celeriac, discolors quickly, so add it to the dressing as you cut each slice. This salad holds well overnight in the refrigerator.

SUN-DRIED TOMATO DRESSING

¼	cup prepared *Mayonnaise* (page 48)
¼	cup sour cream
¼	cup oil-packed sun-dried tomatoes, drained, chopped
2	tablespoons minced fresh chives
2	teaspoons grated lemon peel
1	tablespoon fresh lemon juice
2	teaspoons Dijon mustard

SALAD

1	celery root, about 4 inches in diameter
4	cups arugula leaves, washed thoroughly, drained well
2	tablespoons extra-virgin olive oil
½	teaspoon salt
¼	teaspoon freshly ground pepper

❶ In large bowl, combine Mayonnaise, sour cream, sun-dried tomatoes, chives, lemon peel, lemon juice and mustard. Whisk until smooth.

❷ Peel and halve celery root. Cut each half into ⅛-inch-thick slices. Using mandoline or sharp knife, cut slices into thin, matchstick-size pieces, about 2 inches long. As they are cut, stir celery root slices into dressing.

❸ Toss arugula with olive oil, salt and pepper; divide among 4 salad plates. Top each plate of arugula with about ¾ cup Celery Root Salad. (Salad can be prepared up to 24 hours ahead. Cover and refrigerate; bring to room temperature before serving.)

4 servings.

Preparation time: 40 minutes. Ready to serve: 40 minutes.

Per serving: 220 calories, 20 g total fat (4 g saturated fat), 20 mg cholesterol, 455 mg sodium, 1.5 g fiber.

ASPARAGUS WITH SWEET RED PEPPER DRESSING

In Europe, everything seems to come to a halt when the first asparagus arrives in the market. It's the time to sit down with a giant platter of thick stems and eat them with your fingers. The thickest stems are the tastiest. Be sure to choose those without any woodiness showing at the stem end. They should be green from top to bottom.

2	roasted red bell peppers
2	garlic cloves, chopped
2	tablespoons fresh oregano
2	teaspoons fresh lemon juice
½	teaspoon salt
⅓	cup olive oil
1	lb. fresh asparagus
½	cup (2 oz.) crumbled soft goat cheese

❶ In blender, combine bell peppers, garlic, oregano, lemon juice and salt. Cover; blend until smooth. With blender running, add olive oil in a steady stream. (Pepper puree can be prepared up to 24 hours ahead. Cover and refrigerate; bring to room temperature before serving.)

❷ Break tough ends from asparagus. Using vegetable peeler, peel asparagus from just below flowering top to the end.

❸ Fill skillet with water. Bring to a boil over high heat; add asparagus. Cook 5 minutes or until tender. Drain; run asparagus under cold water to stop cooking.

❹ Arrange asparagus on platter or divide among 4 plates. Drizzle each serving with about ¼ cup dressing; sprinkle with goat cheese.

4 servings.

Preparation time: 15 minutes. Ready to serve: 25 minutes.

Per serving: 240 calories, 20 g total fat (4.5 g saturated fat), 10 mg cholesterol, 345 mg sodium, 2.5 g fiber.

RED PEPPER, FENNEL, ORANGE AND ONION SALAD

Slightly sweet with honey and oranges, and slightly sour with dry-cured Kalamata olives, this salad combines traditional Mediterranean ingredients. The beautiful presentation will grace a buffet of grilled lamb, chicken and fish ... or add a delightful Mediterranean touch to almost any meal.

2 large red bell peppers, cut into thin strips	1 teaspoon ground coriander
1 bulb fennel, white part only, cut into thin strips	1 teaspoon ground ginger
1 red onion, halved, cut into thin slices	½ cup fresh orange juice
2 tablespoons olive oil	2 tablespoons honey
½ teaspoon salt	1 tablespoon soy sauce
2 oranges, peeled, white pith cut away, cut into slices	2 garlic cloves, minced
1 tablespoon sesame seeds	1 tablespoon sesame oil
	½ lb. mixed greens
	1 cup dry-cured Kalamata olives

❶ Heat oven to 375°F. Spread bell peppers, fennel and onion on large shallow baking sheet. Drizzle with olive oil; sprinkle with ¼ teaspoon of the salt. Toss to coat. Bake until softened but not darkened, about 30 minutes, stirring once. Place in ceramic or glass dish. Top with orange slices.

❷ In small saucepan over medium heat, toast sesame seeds. Add coriander and ginger; stir. Heat until fragrant. Add orange juice, honey, soy sauce, garlic and remaining ¼ teaspoon salt. Bring to a boil; reduce heat. Simmer until slightly thickened, about 5 minutes. Let cool slightly. Stir in sesame oil; pour over vegetables and oranges. Gently toss to coat. Cover; let stand at room temperature 2 hours. (Salad can be prepared to this point up to 24 hours ahead. Cover and refrigerate.)

❸ To serve, arrange greens on large platter or divide among 6 plates. Top with vegetable and orange mixture. Sprinkle with olives. If desired, serve with warm pita bread or flatbread.

6 servings.

Preparation time: 30 minutes. Ready to serve: 3 hours.

Per serving: 190 calories, 10.5 g total fat (1.5 g saturated fat), 0 mg cholesterol, 605 mg sodium, 5 g fiber.

BEETS AND ORANGES

This colorful salad with contrasting flavor, color and texture is very Mediterranean in style. As it sits, the flavors become better and better. Beets and Oranges *also makes a beautiful addition to a buffet table or potluck.*

1 lb. red beets, stems trimmed to 1 inch above beets
¼ cup water
2 oranges
1 teaspoon ground cumin
½ teaspoon ground cardamom
½ teaspoon ground coriander
½ teaspoon salt
¼ teaspoon freshly ground pepper
1 tablespoon fresh lemon juice
2 tablespoons extra-virgin olive oil
½ cup (2 oz.) feta cheese, crumbled

❶ Heat oven to 400°F. Place beets in 13x9-inch pan; add water. Cover with aluminum foil; bake 45 minutes to 1 hour or until tender. Let cool. Cut stem and root from beets; peel and slice.

❷ Meanwhile, using sharp knife, peel oranges, cutting away all white pulp and thin outer membrane. Holding over bowl to catch juice, cut between inner membranes to loosen and remove segments. Reserve orange segments and ¼ cup juice.

❸ In small skillet, toast cumin, cardamom and coriander over low heat until fragrant. Stir spices, salt, pepper and lemon juice into reserved ¼ cup orange juice. Pour mixture over beets; gently stir. Drizzle beets with olive oil; gently stir. (Beets can be prepared up to 24 hours ahead. Cover and refrigerate; bring to room temperature before serving.)

❹ Arrange sliced beets and reserved orange segments on platter or 4 salad plates. Sprinkle with feta. Pour marinade from beets into small pitcher. Serve alongside salad.

4 servings.

Preparation time: 30 minutes. Ready to serve: 1 hour, 45 minutes.

Per serving: 165 calories, 10 g total fat (3 g saturated fat), 10 mg cholesterol, 510 mg sodium, 3 g fiber.

SHAVED BEET SALAD WITH CHARDONNAY VINAIGRETTE

This is a beautiful salad with tender, small, yellow and pretty Chioggia beets with their pink and white spirals. Reduced wine vinaigrettes are wine-friendly, so don't be afraid to serve a crisp white wine.

½ cup Chardonnay or dry white wine
2 tablespoons minced shallots
¼ teaspoon salt
¼ teaspoon freshly ground pepper
¼ cup extra-virgin olive oil
1 Chioggia beet or 1 small red beet
1 small yellow beet
½ small bulb fennel
9 cups (12 oz.) mixed spring greens
½ cup (2 oz.) crumbled goat cheese
6 tablespoons prepared *Sugar-Spiced Walnuts* (page 32)

❶ In small saucepan, combine wine and shallots. Bring to a simmer over medium heat. Simmer until wine is reduced to ¼ cup, about 5 minutes. Stir in salt and pepper. Let cool slightly. Whisk in olive oil.

❷ Using vegetable peeler or mandoline, cut beets and fennel into paper-thin slices. Place each vegetable in separate bowl; toss each with about 1 tablespoon of the dressing.

❸ Just before serving, place handful of greens on each of 6 salad plates. Drizzle each with about 1 tablespoon dressing. Arrange beet and fennel slices over greens. Sprinkle each serving with crumbled goat cheese and Sugar-Spiced Walnuts.

6 servings.

Preparation time: 30 minutes. Ready to serve: 45 minutes.

Per serving: 190 calories, 15 g total fat (3 g saturated fat), 10 mg cholesterol, 205 mg sodium, 2.5 g fiber.

SUCCOTASH SALAD

Warm or at room temperature, Succotash Salad partners perfectly with grilled meat or chicken. The flavor is even more delicious when refrigerated overnight. Allow salad to come to room temperature, or microwave on High about 2 minutes to take off the chill.

1   tablespoon olive oil
2   small red onions, cut into 1-inch pieces
6   garlic cloves, halved
½   cup cream
½   teaspoon salt
½   teaspoon freshly ground pepper
3   cups fresh corn kernels or 2 (15-oz.) cans whole kernel corn, drained
1   cup frozen lima beans, thawed under running water 1 minute
1   red bell pepper, cut into 1-inch pieces
⅓   cup fresh mint, torn

❶ Heat oven to 375°F. Brush baking sheet with olive oil. Top with onions and garlic; stir to lightly coat with oil. Bake 20 minutes or until tender; let cool.

❷ In blender, combine 1 cup of the onion mixture, cream, salt and ground pepper. Cover; blend until smooth.

❸ In large bowl, combine remaining onion mixture, corn, lima beans, bell pepper and mint; toss to mix well. Add dressing; toss again. Cover; let stand 1 hour to allow flavors to blend. (Salad can be prepared up to 24 hours ahead. Cover and refrigerate; bring to room temperature before serving.)

6 (¾-cup) servings.

Preparation time: 30 minutes. Ready to serve: 1 hour, 30 minutes.

Per serving: 190 calories, 9 g total fat (4 g saturated fat), 20 mg cholesterol, 220 mg sodium, 5 g fiber.

CHEF'S NOTE

• In the summer, when fava beans are in the market, use them in place of lima beans. Shell 2 pounds of fava beans. Add beans to boiling water and cook 2 minutes. Drain and cover with ice water. Peel each bean by pinching off one end of the skin and gently squeezing out the bean.

CRISP SLAW WITH HOT BACON DRESSING

What a terrific change from mayonnaise-based coleslaw! The hot dressing tossed with cool cabbage tastes wonderful with a hot pastrami sandwich or piled next to sautéed bratwurst or kielbasa.

3	cups shredded red cabbage (about ½ medium cabbage)
3	cups shredded green cabbage (about ½ medium cabbage)
¼	cup (2 oz.) diced lean bacon
¼	cup finely chopped onion
1	tablespoon all-purpose flour
¼	cup water
3	tablespoons cider vinegar
2	tablespoons hot mustard
2	tablespoons packed brown sugar
¼	teaspoon salt

❶ In large bowl, combine red and green cabbage; toss well.

❷ In saucepan over medium heat, combine bacon and onion. Cook over medium heat, stirring occasionally, until bacon is crisp and onion is tender, about 5 minutes.

❸ Sprinkle bacon mixture with flour. Cook, stirring constantly, 1 minute. Remove from heat. Stir in water, vinegar, mustard, brown sugar and salt until well blended. Return to heat. Cook, stirring constantly, about 1 minute or until mixture has thickened slightly.

❹ Pour hot dressing over cabbage; toss to mix well. Serve while warm.

6 (¾-cup) servings.

Preparation time: 20 minutes. Ready to serve: 31 minutes.

Per serving: 105 calories, 6.5 g total fat (2.5 g saturated fat), 5 mg cholesterol, 220 mg sodium, 2 g fiber.

CHEF'S NOTE

• Dressing can be made ahead, covered and refrigerated until serving time. Just before serving, heat dressing in microwave on High 30 seconds. Toss with shredded cabbage.

CAPRESE

Caprese *comes to life in summer with a variety of heirloom tomatoes; it is most colorful with green zebra, Brandywine and bright yellow varieties. Tomatoes and mozzarella become a light entrée salad when arranged on polenta triangles.*

1   quart water
1½ teaspoons salt
1   cup instant polenta*
1   lb. tomatoes, a mixture of yellow, red and green, if available, thickly sliced
1   cup fresh basil, torn
2   tablespoons extra-virgin olive oil
½   teaspoon freshly ground pepper
1   lb. fresh mozzarella (Italian buffalo mozzarella, if available), thinly sliced

❶ Lightly grease 13x9-inch pan.

❷ In large saucepan over medium heat, bring water and 1 teaspoon of the salt to a boil. Slowly whisk in polenta. Reduce heat to lowest possible heat; cook, stirring constantly, 5 to 10 minutes or until mixture thickens and polenta begins to pull away from sides of saucepan.

❸ Pour mixture into prepared pan; let stand until firm, about 5 minutes.

❹ Cut polenta into fourths. Cut each fourth in half to create a total of 12 triangles.

❺ Place 2 polenta triangles on each of 6 plates. Arrange tomatoes over polenta. Sprinkle with basil, olive oil, remaining salt and pepper. Top with mozzarella. Sprinkle with any remaining basil, oil, salt and pepper.

6 servings.

Preparation time: 30 minutes. Ready to serve: 35 minutes.

Per serving: 355 calories, 24 g total fat (11 g saturated fat), 55 mg cholesterol, 965 mg sodium, 2.5 g fiber.

TIP *Polenta splatters as it thickens, and can burn you. Hold a screen or lid partially over the pot as you stir.

MEAT, FISH & CHICKEN SALADS

Comfort food in a salad! Many of the salads in this chapter are inspired by old favorites; they're just in a different form. Some are terrific followed by a light entrée. Others are the entrée. Serve one of these salads with al fresco dinners, summer lunches or any time a one-dish meal is called for. Just add dessert for a complete meal.

White Bean and Beef Salad with Tiny Cherry Tomatoes, page 93

CHICKEN FAJITA SALAD

Don't let the long ingredient list prevent you from making this big, one-plate meal. Everything is just tossed together, taking very little time. For a lighter alternative to fried tortilla strips, serve the salad with fresh, warm tortillas.

LIME VINAIGRETTE
¼ cup fresh lime juice
¼ cup extra-virgin olive oil
2 garlic cloves, minced
¾ teaspoon salt
¼ teaspoon freshly ground pepper

SALAD
¼ cup vegetable oil
2 corn tortillas, cut into thin strips*
½ teaspoon salt
1 (15- to 16-oz.) can black beans, drained, rinsed
2 cups fresh corn kernels or 1 (15- to 16-oz.) can whole kernel corn, drained
1 large tomato, seeded, diced
1 large jalapeño chile, minced (include seeds if you like it hotter)
¼ cup finely chopped fresh cilantro
6 cups torn iceberg lettuce
2 cups shredded cooked chicken
2 avocados, cut into wedges
1 lime, cut into 8 wedges

GARNISH
Chili powder

❶ In small bowl or pitcher, combine lime juice, olive oil, garlic, ¾ teaspoon salt and pepper. In large skillet, heat oil over medium-high heat until hot. Add just enough tortilla strips to float comfortably. Fry 2 minutes or until crisp. Remove to plate covered with 2 layers of paper towels. Sprinkle with ¼ teaspoon of the salt. Repeat with remaining tortillas and salt.

❷ In large bowl, combine beans, corn, tomato, jalapeño and cilantro. Add ¼ of the dressing; toss well. In another large bowl, combine lettuce and remaining dressing; toss well. Line platter or 4 dinner plates with lettuce. Top with bean mixture. Arrange chicken on top of bean mixture. Sprinkle with tortilla strips. Garnish with avocado and lime wedges. Sprinkle with chili powder.

4 servings.

Preparation time: 20 minutes. Ready to serve: 20 minutes.

Per serving: 670 calories, 39 g total fat (6.5 g saturated fat), 55 mg cholesterol, 1000 mg sodium, 15 g fiber.

TIP *You can use packaged tortilla chips in place of fried tortilla strips.

VIETNAMESE-INSPIRED FISH SALAD

The Vietnamese eat a healthy diet brimming with fresh vegetables and seafood. Flavor comes not from fat, but from herbs, chiles and fish sauce. Fish sauce can be found in the Asian section of supermarkets.

1 lb. red snapper fillets (2 large or 4 small fillets)

¼ cup fresh lime juice

2 tablespoons sugar

2 tablespoons fish sauce

1 garlic clove, minced

½ teaspoon ground white pepper

3 green onions, cut into matchstick-size strips (⅛x⅛x1-inch)

3 serrano chiles, halved lengthwise, seeded and cut into matchstick-size strips (⅛x⅛x1-inch)

½ carrot, peeled, cut into matchstick-size strips (⅛x⅛x1-inch)

2 teaspoons grated fresh ginger

1 head red leaf lettuce, separated into leaves

2 cups bean sprouts, tips removed

1 cup fresh cilantro, torn

½ cup dry-roasted peanuts or cashews

❶ Place fish on heatproof plate that fits in bamboo steamer or on metal biscuit cutter set in covered skillet. In small bowl or pitcher, combine lime juice, sugar, fish sauce, garlic and pepper. Drizzle ½ of the lime juice mixture over fish. Sprinkle green onions, chiles, carrot and ginger over fish.

❷ Place plate with fish in steamer basket set over boiling water in wok or skillet. Cover; steam 10 minutes or until fish is opaque throughout. Line 4 salad plates or a platter with lettuce. Sprinkle with sprouts and cilantro; top with fish. Sprinkle with remaining lime juice mixture and peanuts.

4 servings.

Preparation time: 30 minutes. Ready to serve: 40 minutes.

Per serving: 320 calories, 13 g total fat (2 g saturated fat), 60 mg cholesterol, 585 mg sodium, 6 g fiber.

CHEF'S NOTE

• Asian dishes benefit from special attention to preparation details. For example, use a vegetable peeler to thinly slice the carrot. Stack the slices and cut into thin lengthwise strips. To prepare bean sprouts, pinch off the bulbous seed end and remove the tiny hair at the tip of each sprout.

SMOKED TROUT SALAD WITH PINK GRAPEFRUIT AND AVOCADOS

The raspberry vinaigrette (see below) creates little droplets of jewel tones because the oil is lightly mixed with the vinegar, not blended in. This separation lends lots of great flavor contrast.

VINAIGRETTE
- 3 tablespoons prepared *Raspberry Vinegar* (page 30)
- 3 tablespoons hazelnut oil or walnut oil
- 1 tablespoon minced shallot
- 1½ teaspoons grated fresh ginger
- ½ teaspoon salt
- ⅛ teaspoon ground white pepper

SALAD
- 1 large head frisee (curly endive)
- 1 pink grapefruit
- 3 oz. hot-smoked trout or salmon, flaked*
- 2 avocados, peeled, sliced

❶ In small bowl or pitcher, combine Raspberry Vinegar, oil, shallot, ginger, salt and pepper.

❷ Separate frisee leaves; wash well and pat dry. Using sharp knife, peel grapefruit, cutting away all white pulp and thin outer membrane. Holding over bowl to catch juice, cut between inner membranes to remove segments. Cut each segment into 1-inch pieces.

❸ In large bowl, combine frisee, grapefruit segments and ⅓ cup of the dressing; toss well. Arrange on platter or individual salad plates. Top each serving with smoked fish and avocado. Drizzle with remaining dressing.

6 servings.

Preparation time: 20 minutes. Ready to serve: 30 minutes.

Per serving: 200 calories, 16.5 g total fat (2 g saturated fat), 5 mg cholesterol, 235 mg sodium, 6.5 g fiber.

TIP *Hot-smoked fish is usually sold in a chunk and flakes easily. Cold-smoked fish is smooth and not flaky and is often sold thinly sliced. Both are delicious, and either works well in this salad.

HOT PASTRAMI SALAD

You can think of this as a salad or as a make-it-yourself sandwich. Either way, it's reminiscent of a New York deli.

HONEY MUSTARD DRESSING
⅓ cup cider vinegar
¼ cup sweet hot mustard
¼ cup honey
2 teaspoons prepared horseradish (optional)
½ teaspoon salt

SALAD
6 cups chopped iceberg lettuce
8 oz. thinly sliced pastrami, cut into strips, warmed if desired
1 cup miniature pretzels
8 dill pickle spears
4 slices toasted rye bread, each cut in half

❶ In small bowl or pitcher, combine vinegar, mustard, honey, horseradish and salt.

❷ In large bowl, combine lettuce and ¼ cup of the dressing; toss well. Divide lettuce among 4 salad plates.

❸ Arrange pastrami over lettuce. Drizzle each serving with 1 tablespoon dressing. Sprinkle with pretzels. Garnish each plate with 2 pickle spears and 2 halves rye toast.

4 servings.

Preparation time: 15 minutes. Ready to serve: 15 minutes.

Per serving: 380 calories, 18.5 g total fat (6 g saturated fat), 50 mg cholesterol, 2140 mg sodium, 4 g fiber.

$\mathcal{L}$OX AND BAGEL SALAD

Served as a canapé with Champagne or on a bagel to enjoy with the Sunday paper, smoked salmon always holds the center of attention. For a gathering, multiply the ingredients and serve on a large platter.

CREAM CHEESE DRESSING

- ¾ cup (6 oz.) whipped cream cheese
- 2 tablespoons milk
- ¼ teaspoon salt
- ⅛ teaspoon freshly ground pepper
- 2 tablespoons snipped fresh chives

SALAD

- 1 head Boston (bibb) lettuce, separated into leaves, washed and drained
- 4 oz. thinly sliced smoked salmon, shredded
- ½ red onion, cut in half, very thinly sliced
- 2 tomatoes, cut in half, very thinly sliced
- 1 cup (1½ oz.) packaged garlic-flavored bagel chips*

❶ In blender, combine cream cheese, milk, salt and pepper. Cover; blend until smooth. Pour into small bowl; stir in chives. Cover; refrigerate until serving.

❷ Line plates with lettuce. Drizzle each serving with 1 tablespoon of the dressing. (Dressing may be prepared, covered and refrigerated up to 1 day before serving.)

❸ Arrange salmon, onion and tomatoes on top of lettuce; drizzle with remaining dressing. Sprinkle with bagel chips.

4 (¾-cup) servings.

Preparation time: 30 minutes. Ready to serve: 30 minutes.

Per serving: 255 calories, 18 g total fat (10 g saturated fat), 55 mg cholesterol, 555 mg sodium, 2 g fiber.

TIP *If bagel chips are unavailable, substitute 1 onion bagel, cut crosswise into very thin slices. Bake in single layer on baking sheet at 375°F for 5 minutes or until crisp.

LEMON SHRIMP SALAD

This pretty salad is perfect for a spring luncheon.

LEMON DRESSING
2 teaspoons grated lemon peel
3 tablespoons fresh lemon juice
1 tablespoon finely chopped fresh mint
¼ teaspoon salt
⅛ teaspoon freshly ground pepper
¹⁄₁₆ teaspoon sugar
¼ cup extra-virgin olive oil

SALAD
¾ lb. shelled, deveined cooked jumbo shrimp, tails on
1 head frisee (curly endive)
½ cup fresh basil, torn
¼ cup dried cherries or cranberries

❶ In small bowl or pitcher, combine lemon peel, lemon juice, mint, salt, pepper and sugar. Whisk in olive oil.

❷ In medium bowl, combine shrimp and ¼ cup of the dressing; toss.

❸ Separate frisee leaves; wash well and pat dry. In large bowl, combine frisee and basil. Add remaining dressing; toss.

❹ Line 4 salad plates or a platter with frisee mixture; top with shrimp mixture. Sprinkle each serving with 1 tablespoon dried cherries.

4 servings.

Preparation time: 15 minutes. Ready to serve: 15 minutes.

Per serving: 240 calories, 15 g total fat (2 g saturated fat), 165 mg cholesterol, 360 mg sodium, 3.5 g fiber.

CHEF'S NOTE
• When using freshly grated lemon peel and lemon juice, always grate peel from the lemon before juicing. If you always grate peel from any lemon you juice, freeze the peel in small resealable plastic bags.

OVEN-FRIED ROCK SHRIMP WITH CHOPPED VEGETABLES

Rock shrimp are a real treat. Not only do they have a wonderful flavor, but they need no peeling. On menus you may see "popcorn shrimp"; these are fried rock shrimp. Try this oven-fried method for a healthy alternative.

2   cups fresh corn kernels or 1 (15- to 16-oz.) can whole kernel corn, drained
1   green bell pepper, chopped
1   red bell pepper, chopped
1   tomato, seeded, chopped
1   rib celery, chopped
½   cup prepared tartar sauce
6   cups torn red leaf lettuce
¼   cup cornmeal
2   tablespoons all-purpose flour
2   teaspoons chili powder
1   teaspoon kosher (coarse) salt
⅛   teaspoon freshly ground pepper
½   lb. rock shrimp, rinsed, drained and dried with clean towel
1   tablespoon vegetable oil
1   lemon cut into 8 small wedges

❶ Heat oven to 500°F.

❷ In large bowl, combine corn, green and red bell peppers, tomato and celery. Stir in tartar sauce; refrigerate until serving. (This may be done up to 24 hours in advance.)

❸ To serve, line 4 salad plates with lettuce; top each with ¾ cup corn mixture.

❹ In bowl, combine cornmeal, flour, chili powder, salt and pepper. In another bowl, toss shrimp with oil. Stir in flour mixture; toss to coat shrimp.

❺ On baking sheet, arrange shrimp in a single layer. Bake 5 minutes; turn shrimp. Bake an additional 5 to 6 minutes or until shrimp turn pink. Arrange shrimp over corn mixture. Garnish with lemon wedges. Serve immediately.

4 servings.

Preparation time: 15 minutes. Ready to serve: 25 minutes.

Per serving: 370 calories, 20 g total fat (3 g saturated fat), 95 mg cholesterol, 695 mg sodium, 6.5 g fiber.

CLASSIC CHEF'S SALAD

This classic salad is popular because there's so much variety on one plate. With the ever-expanding selection of meats and cheeses in markets, you can always alter and update this salad to your liking.

GORGONZOLA DRESSING
- ½ cup prepared *Mayonnaise* (page 48)
- ½ cup softened Gorgonzola or Roquefort cheese, crumbled
- 2 tablespoons cream or milk

CHEF'S SALAD
- 1 head romaine lettuce
- 2 cups (8 oz.) diced fontina or Gruyère cheese
- 2 cups (8 oz.) diced Black Forest ham
- 2 cups (8 oz.) diced smoked turkey or chicken
- 3 small red tomatoes, diced
- 3 small yellow tomatoes, diced
- 3 hard-cooked eggs, quartered lengthwise (see Chef's Note, page 129)

❶ In medium bowl, combine Mayonnaise, Gorgonzola and cream, leaving some chunks in the dressing. Cover; refrigerate while arranging salads.

❷ Cut lettuce just above core. Place in large bowl of ice water; soak 5 minutes. Drain well. Cut lettuce crosswise into 1-inch pieces.

❸ Mound about 1½ cups lettuce on each of 6 salad plates. Arrange fontina, ham, turkey and red and yellow tomatoes in pie-shaped wedges on top of each lettuce mound.

❹ Arrange quartered eggs around edges of plates. Top each salad with about 2 tablespoons dressing.

6 servings.

Preparation time: 30 minutes. Ready to serve: 30 minutes.

Per serving: 480 calories, 35 g total fat (14.5 g saturated fat), 210 mg cholesterol, 1530 mg sodium, 2.5 g fiber.

CHEF'S NOTE

• Use a strongly flavored blue cheese in the dressing since it will be "cut" with Mayonnaise. In the salad, use a cheese that will stand up to, but not clash with, the blue cheese.

WHITE BEAN AND BEEF SALAD WITH TINY CHERRY TOMATOES

White beans, spiked with plenty of garlic and herbs, make a delicious background for grilled steak. Leftover grilled beef is perfect in this salad.

 12 oz. flank steak
1½ teaspoons salt
 ½ teaspoon freshly ground pepper
  2 (16-oz.) cans white beans, drained, rinsed
  1 cup Sweet 100 cherry tomatoes or 2 cups regular cherry tomatoes, quartered
  ¼ red onion, finely chopped
  ¼ cup extra-virgin olive oil
  2 tablespoons chopped fresh oregano
  1 tablespoon chopped fresh thyme
  2 tablespoons red wine vinegar
  2 garlic cloves, minced

❶ Heat grill or broiler. Season steak on both sides with ½ teaspoon of the salt and ¼ teaspoon of the pepper. Cook steak 4 to 6 inches from heat, turning once during cooking, about 10 minutes or until medium-rare. Let cool 10 minutes; slice thinly. Pull slices into shreds.

❷ In large bowl, combine beans, tomatoes, onion, olive oil, oregano, thyme, vinegar, garlic, remaining 1 teaspoon salt and ¼ teaspoon pepper. Add steak; toss. May be served immediately or marinated 1 hour at room temperature. (Salad can be prepared up to 24 hours ahead. Cover and refrigerate; bring to room temperature before serving.)

6 (1-cup) servings.

Preparation time: 20 minutes. Ready to serve: 40 minutes.

Per serving: 320 calories, 13.5 g total fat (3 g saturated fat), 30 mg cholesterol, 475 mg sodium, 7 g fiber.

PASTA SALADS

Pasta has many wonderful variations. Soba noodles, rice sticks and couscous are just a few of the international offerings besides the myriad Italian pasta shapes. Pasta salads are at their finest when served at room temperature. Refrigerate leftovers, but bring them back to room temperature before serving. When cooking Italian-style pasta, abundantly salt the cooking water. Since it's eventually drained off, it doesn't add much salt to your dish, but it really flavors the pasta inside and out.

Pasta Salad with a Trio of Roasted Chiles, page 107

CHICKEN NOODLE SALAD

Here's a comfortingly familiar salad based on the ingredients in chicken noodle soup. This can be served cold or slightly warmed for a hearty entrée.

1	tablespoon kosher (coarse) salt
1	(8-oz.) pkg. angel hair pasta
2	tablespoons vegetable oil
1	cup sour cream
2	teaspoons grated lemon peel
1	tablespoon fresh lemon juice
½	teaspoon kosher (coarse) salt
¼	teaspoon freshly ground pepper
1	cup shredded cooked chicken
¼	cup finely chopped onion, soaked in ice water 5 minutes, drained
¼	cup finely chopped carrot
¼	cup finely chopped celery
2	tablespoons chopped fresh Italian parsley
1	tablespoon chopped fresh thyme (use lemon thyme, if available)

❶ Fill large pot ⅔ full of water; add kosher salt. Bring to a boil over high heat. Add pasta; cook 8 to 10 minutes or until al dente. Drain, reserving ¼ cup cooking water. Rinse thoroughly in cool water; drain. Transfer pasta to large bowl; toss with oil and reserved cooking water.

❷ In small bowl, combine sour cream, lemon peel, lemon juice, ½ teaspoon salt and pepper. Add sour cream mixture to pasta; toss to mix well. Add chicken, onion, carrot, celery, parsley and thyme; toss again.

6 servings.

Preparation time: 30 minutes. Ready to serve: 40 minutes.

Per serving: 315 calories, 14.5 g total fat (5.5 g saturated fat), 45 mg cholesterol, 385 mg sodium, 2 g fiber.

SUMMER GARDEN SALAD

Making this salad may become a summer ritual when the best of the produce is at its peak. The vegetables don't really need to be cooked, just "licked" with the flames until golden brown, creating a toasty-sweet flavor.

1 cob corn, husks and silk removed
1 small red onion, quartered
2 firm tomatoes (use heirloom tomatoes, if available)
1 tablespoon plus 1 teaspoon kosher (coarse) salt
1 (8-oz.) pkg. corkscrew pasta (fusilli)
¾ cup fresh basil, torn
3 garlic cloves
¼ teaspoon freshly ground pepper
¼ teaspoon white wine vinegar
¼ cup extra-virgin olive oil
1 recipe prepared *Crostini* (page 35)

❶ Heat grill. Cook corn and onion 4 to 6 inches from heat, turning occasionally, 10 minutes. Add tomatoes to grill. Cook 5 minutes or just until slightly softened but not cooked through, turning occasionally. Remove from grill; let cool.

❷ Meanwhile, fill large pot ⅔ full of water; add 1 tablespoon of the salt. Bring to a boil over high heat. Add pasta; cook 15 minutes or until al dente. Drain. Rinse thoroughly in cool water; drain. Transfer to large bowl.

❸ Cut kernels from corn; cut onion into 1-inch pieces. Peel tomatoes; seed and coarsely chop. In large bowl, combine pasta, corn, onion, tomatoes and basil; toss well.

❹ Using mortar and pestle or side of chef's knife, mash garlic, remaining 1 teaspoon salt and pepper into a paste; transfer to small bowl. Stir in vinegar; mix well. Gradually whisk in olive oil. Add to pasta mixture; toss. Serve with Crostini.

6 (1-cup) servings.

Preparation time: 15 minutes. Ready to serve: 45 minutes.

Per serving: 505 calories, 17.5 g total fat (2.5 g saturated fat), 0 mg cholesterol, 900 mg sodium, 5 g fiber.

SOBA NOODLE SALAD WITH PAPAYAS, RED ONION AND CILANTRO

Miso, made from fermented soybeans, has long been a healthy staple in Japanese cooking. Use lighter miso for a more delicate flavor, darker for a fuller flavor.

1   (8-oz.) pkg. soba (buckwheat) noodles
3   tablespoons vegetable oil
2   tablespoons miso (light or dark)
2   tablespoons seasoned rice vinegar
1   garlic clove, minced
½   teaspoon crushed red pepper
½   papaya, peeled, cut into thin wedges (about 1 cup)
½   cup chopped red onion
¼   cup fresh cilantro, torn
2   tablespoons toasted sesame seeds

❶ Fill large pot ⅔ full of water. Bring to a boil over high heat. Add soba noodles; cook 2 to 3 minutes or just until tender. Drain. Rinse thoroughly in cool water; drain. Transfer to large bowl.

❷ In small bowl, combine oil, miso, vinegar, garlic and crushed red pepper. Add to soba noodles; toss well. Gently stir in papaya, onion and cilantro.

❸ Cover and refrigerate at least 1 hour, but no longer than 4 hours.* Sprinkle with sesame seeds before serving.

6 (1-cup) servings.

Preparation time: 30 minutes. Ready to serve: 1 hour, 30 minutes.

Per serving: 225 calories, 9.5 g total fat (1.5 g saturated fat), 0 mg cholesterol, 215 mg sodium, 5.5 g fiber.

TIP *To hold 4 to 24 hours, add papaya just before serving.

CREAMY PENNE WITH TUNA AND CAPERS

This easy-to-make pasta salad appeals to kids of all ages. Have a bowl of it on hand for after-school hunger attacks.

1 tablespoon kosher (coarse) salt
1 (8-oz.) pkg. penne
2 tablespoons olive oil
4 oz. light cream cheese, softened
2 tablespoons grated white onion
1 (6-oz.) can olive oil-packed tuna, drained
1 tomato, halved, seeded and finely chopped
3 tablespoons drained capers
¼ cup fresh Italian parsley, torn
½ teaspoon salt
¼ teaspoon freshly ground pepper

❶ Fill large pot ⅔ full of water; add kosher salt. Bring to a boil over high heat. Add penne; cook 10 minutes or until al dente. Drain, reserving ¼ cup cooking water. Rinse thoroughly in cool water; drain. Transfer pasta to large bowl; toss with olive oil.

❷ In small bowl, combine reserved cooking water, cream cheese and onion; mix until cream cheese is smooth. Add to pasta; stir to mix well.

❸ Add tuna, tomato, capers, parsley, ½ teaspoon salt and pepper to pasta; stir to mix well. Refrigerate 1 hour to allow flavors to blend.

6 (1-cup) servings.

Preparation time: 10 minutes. Ready to eat: 1 hour, 10 minutes.

Per serving: 290 calories, 11 g total fat (3.5 g saturated fat), 10 mg cholesterol, 660 mg sodium, 2 g fiber.

CHEF'S NOTE

• Whole herb leaves, such as flat-leaf parsley, cilantro and oregano, are pretty and delicious in salads. To remove leaves quickly, give your herbs a "haircut." Leaving the herbs in a bunch, wash and trim stems to about ½ inch. Using sharp, pointed scissors, cut off as many leaves as you need at one time. The herbs, stored like a bouquet in a glass of water, will keep in the refrigerator several days.

ONIONS

When using any of the onion varieties in their raw state for salads, cover chopped onion with ice-cold water for at least 5 minutes before adding to the finished dish. This removes some of the strongest onion flavor.

White onions are strongly flavored, but are often enjoyed raw in fresh salsas and sprinkled into salads; they are a staple in Mexican cooking.

Yellow onions, available year-round as storage onions, are used most frequently for cooking.

Red onions are beautiful and can be sweet when fresh. Choose Spanish onions and torpedo onions if they're in the market. Red onions add beautiful color to grilled, mixed vegetable salads, and are delicious when thinly sliced and tossed with cucumber and seasoned rice vinegar.

Sweet, fresh onions are wonderful raw, grilled and roasted. They are shipped fresh, so many of the sweet varieties are seasonal. Depending upon your region and the time of year you may see Maui, Vidalia, Texas 1015s, Super Sweet and Walla Walla, among others. Grated onion is good when the flavor of raw onion should be mixed evenly into a salad or salad dressing.

PEPPER PASTA SALAD WITH BASIL VINAIGRETTE

Colorful and light, this salad could become a regular on your menu. It's a perfect accompaniment to simply prepared chops, fish or chicken. Turn Pepper Pasta Salad with Basil Vinaigrette *into an entrée by adding fresh mozzarella or poached salmon.*

BASIL VINAIGRETTE

- ¼ cup fresh basil, torn
- 2 tablespoons chopped shallots
- 1 tablespoon white wine vinegar
- ½ teaspoon kosher (coarse) salt
- ¼ teaspoon freshly ground pepper
- ⅓ cup extra-virgin olive oil

PASTA SALAD

- 1 tablespoon kosher (coarse) salt
- 1 (8-oz.) pkg. penne
- 2 roasted red bell peppers, coarsely chopped
- 2 roasted yellow bell peppers, coarsely chopped
- 2 cups loosely packed baby arugula

❶ In blender, combine basil, shallots, vinegar, ½ teaspoon salt and pepper. Cover; blend until smooth. With blender running, gradually add olive oil.

❷ Meanwhile, fill large pot ⅔ full of water; add kosher salt. Bring to a boil over high heat. Add penne; cook 10 minutes or until al dente. Drain. Rinse thoroughly in cool water; drain. Transfer to large bowl.

❸ Combine vinaigrette and pasta; toss well. Add roasted peppers and arugula; toss again. (Salad can be prepared up to 24 hours ahead. Cover and refrigerate; bring to room temperature before serving.)

6 (1-cup) servings.

Preparation time: 10 minutes. Ready to serve: 25 minutes.

Per serving: 270 calories, 13 g total fat (2 g saturated fat), 0 mg cholesterol, 345 mg sodium, 2.5 g fiber.

CHEF'S NOTE

• To prepare quickly, use 1¼ cups each purchased roasted red and yellow bell peppers.

MEDITERRANEAN COUSCOUS SALAD

Couscous looks like grain, but it's pasta made from semolina flour. Large couscous, called Middle Eastern or Israeli couscous, is becoming more widely available. Pita bread, cut into wedges and crisped in the oven, makes the perfect accompaniment to this salad.

1 tablespoon kosher (coarse) salt
2 cups Israeli (large) couscous
1 (3-inch) cinnamon stick
1 tablespoon cumin seeds
1 tablespoon coriander seeds
¼ cup extra-virgin olive oil
1 tablespoon fresh lemon juice
½ teaspoon kosher (coarse) salt
¼ teaspoon freshly ground pepper
1 *Preserved Lemon*, rinsed, chopped (page 38)
½ cup fresh mint, chopped
½ cup grated carrot
¼ cup chopped green onions

❶ Fill large pot ⅔ full of water; add kosher salt. Bring to a boil over high heat. Add couscous; cook 10 minutes or until al dente. Drain. Rinse thoroughly in cool water; drain. Transfer to large bowl.

❷ In skillet, toast cinnamon stick, cumin seeds and coriander seeds over medium heat until fragrant. Remove from heat; let cool. Grind spices using mortar and pestle or coffee grinder reserved for spices.

❸ In small bowl or pitcher, combine spices, olive oil, lemon juice, ½ teaspoon salt and pepper. Add to couscous; toss well. Add Preserved Lemon, mint, carrot and green onions; toss again.

6 (1-cup) servings.
Preparation time: 15 minutes. Ready to serve: 25 minutes.

Per serving: 265 calories, 10.5 g total fat (1.5 g saturated fat), 0 mg cholesterol, 630 mg sodium, 2.5 g fiber.

ℬEET RED PASTA SALAD

This salad is a mess! But it's also delicious, and worth the trouble. Roast the beets anytime you have the oven on for another purpose. You can refrigerate them for up to two days.

1   lb. red beets, stems trimmed to about 1 inch above beets
¼   cup water
1   tablespoon kosher (coarse) salt
1   (8-oz.) pkg. fettuccine
¼   cup extra-virgin olive oil
2   tablespoons chopped fresh oregano
1   tablespoon chopped fresh marjoram, if available
1   tablespoon balsamic vinegar
¾   teaspoon salt
¼   teaspoon freshly ground pepper
¾   cup (3 oz.) crumbled goat cheese

❶ Heat oven to 400°F. Place beets in casserole; add water. Cover with aluminum foil. Bake 45 minutes to 1 hour or until tender. Let cool. Cut stem and root from beets; peel and quarter.

❷ Meanwhile, fill large pot ⅔ full of water; add kosher salt. Bring to a boil over high heat. Add fettuccine; cook 10 minutes or until al dente. Drain, reserving ½ cup cooking water. Rinse thoroughly in cool water; drain. Transfer to large bowl.

❸ In blender, combine olive oil, oregano, marjoram, balsamic vinegar, ¾ teaspoon salt and pepper. Cover; blend until combined. Add beets to blender. Cover; blend until pureed. Add ¼ to ½ cup pasta cooking water, if necessary, to thin sauce slightly. Add beet dressing to pasta; toss well.

❹ Sprinkle each serving with 2 to 3 tablespoons goat cheese. If desired, sprinkle with pepper and additional fresh oregano and marjoram.

4 (1-cup) servings.

Preparation time: 20 minutes. Ready to serve: 1 hour, 20 minutes.

Per serving: 405 calories, 20.5 g total fat (5.5 g saturated fat), 70 mg cholesterol, 810 mg sodium, 3 g fiber.

RICE STICK SALAD

Noodles without cooking! Rice stick noodles are simply soaked in hot water. Feel free to spice them up with thinly slivered serrano chiles; or add more vegetables, such as cucumber and broccoli.

½ lb. dried flat rice stick noodles, ¼-inch wide*
½ cup chunky peanut butter
¼ cup hot water
2 tablespoons soy sauce
4 teaspoons fresh lime juice

½ teaspoon crushed red pepper
¼ teaspoon salt
⅓ cup chopped green onions
1 cup shredded carrot
¼ cup chopped dry-roasted peanuts

❶ Place noodles in medium bowl; cover with boiling water. Soak 20 minutes or until tender.

❷ Meanwhile, in small bowl, combine peanut butter, ¼ cup hot water, soy sauce, lime juice, crushed red pepper and salt.

❸ Drain noodles; add peanut butter mixture. Stir well to combine. Add green onions and carrot; toss. Sprinkle with peanuts.

6 (1-cup) servings.

Preparation time: 10 minutes. Ready to serve: 30 minutes.

Per serving: 260 calories, 13.5 g total fat (2.5 g saturated fat), 0 mg cholesterol, 575 mg sodium, 3 g fiber.

TIP *Rice stick noodles are found in the Asian section of most large supermarkets.

PASTA SALAD WITH A TRIO OF ROASTED CHILES

Tap into the delicious variety of chiles in today's market. Poblanos, traditionally used for chiles rellenos *(sweet peppers stuffed with a cheese filling, deep-fried and topped with cheese), aren't too spicy, but have a slightly earthy flavor. Mild-mannered Anaheims keep their "crunch" even when roasted, while jalapeños add kick.*

2 poblano chiles
2 Anaheim chiles
2 red jalapeño chiles
1 tablespoon kosher (coarse) salt
1 (8-oz.) pkg. farfalle (bow-tie pasta)
¼ cup olive oil
1 tablespoon chopped fresh oregano
2 tablespoons fresh orange juice
1 tablespoon fresh lime juice
½ teaspoon kosher (coarse) salt
¼ teaspoon freshly ground pepper
2 tablespoons crumbed Mexican cotija cheese* or shredded Parmesan cheese (optional)
6 small lime wedges

❶ Heat grill. Cook chiles 4 to 6 inches from heat, turning occasionally, until charred on all sides, about 5 to 10 minutes. Place in plastic bag to steam; let sit 5 minutes. Peel away charred skin. Cut poblano and Anaheim chiles into 1-inch pieces. Cut jalapeño into ⅛-inch pieces. Set aside.

❷ Fill large pot ⅔ full of water; add kosher salt. Bring to a boil over high heat. Add pasta; cook 15 minutes or until al dente. Drain. Rinse thoroughly in cool water; drain.

❸ Transfer pasta to large bowl. Add olive oil, oregano, orange juice, lime juice, ½ teaspoon salt and ground pepper; toss.

❹ Fold chile peppers into pasta. Sprinkle with cheese, if desired. Serve with lime wedges.

6 (¾-cup) servings.
Preparation time: 15 minutes. Ready to serve: 25 minutes.
Per serving: 265 calories, 10.5 g total fat (1.5 g saturated fat), 5 mg cholesterol, 365 mg sodium, 2.5 g fiber.

TIP* Cotija cheese is a dry, aged Mexican cheese, not unlike Parmesan.

BEAN & GRAIN SALADS

Bean and grain salads are so versatile and flavorful that you'll want to keep a couple of them on hand for snacks and quick side dishes. All the recipes in this chapter benefit from time, which allows the flavors to blend. This means you can prepare them ahead and store for two to three days. Then, when a meal is needed in a hurry, there's always something ready! Serve these salads at room temperature for optimum flavor.

Lentil Salad, page 121

CANNELLINI BEAN SALAD

Often served as an antipasto, cannellini beans and tuna are a favorite combination in many areas of Italy. This version takes advantage of the perfect marriage of parsley, lemon peel and garlic. For the very best flavor, use tuna packed in olive oil.

⅓ cup chopped fresh Italian parsley
2 teaspoons grated lemon peel
2 garlic cloves, minced
½ teaspoon salt
2 (15-oz.) cans cannellini (white) beans, drained, rinsed
1 (6-oz.) can olive oil-packed tuna, drained
3 tablespoons extra-virgin olive oil
1 tablespoon fresh lemon juice

❶ In small bowl, combine parsley, lemon peel, garlic and salt.

❷ In large bowl, combine beans, tuna, olive oil and lemon juice. Add parsley mixture; toss. (Salad can be prepared up to 24 hours ahead. Cover and refrigerate; bring to room temperature before serving.)

6 (¾-cup) servings.

Preparation time: 15 minutes. Ready to serve: 15 minutes.

Per serving: 250 calories, 9 g total fat (1.5 g saturated fat), 5 mg cholesterol, 520 mg sodium, 6.5 g fiber.

Hominy and Broccoli

Yellow, bright green and brilliant red vegetables color this glorious salad. The flavor of the dressing is just as bright with lime juice, cumin, coriander and a hint of hot red pepper.

1 tablespoon each cumin seeds, coriander seeds*	1 red bell pepper, cut into thin strips, 2 inches long
⅛ teaspoon crushed red pepper	¼ cup extra-virgin olive oil
1 (15-oz.) can yellow or white hominy, drained, rinsed	2 teaspoons grated lime peel
2 cups broccoli florets, blanched	2 tablespoons fresh lime juice
	1 teaspoon salt

❶ In skillet, toast cumin seeds, coriander seeds and crushed red pepper over medium heat until fragrant. Remove from heat; let cool. Grind spices using mortar and pestle or coffee grinder reserved for spices.

❷ In large bowl, combine hominy, broccoli and bell pepper. Stir in toasted spices, olive oil, lime peel, lime juice and salt.

4 (¾-cup) servings.

Preparation time: 20 minutes. Ready to serve: 20 minutes.

Per serving: 200 calories, 15 g total fat (2 g saturated fat), 0 mg cholesterol, 750 mg sodium, 3.5 g fiber.

TIP *One teaspoon each ground cumin and ground coriander may be substituted for the seeds. Toast ground spices carefully, as they burn more quickly than seeds.

QUINOA WITH SMOKED CHICKEN

If light, fluffy, versatile, delicious and easy to prepare aren't enough kudos, quinoa is also one of the planet's most healthful foods. This ancient grain is a complete protein and is lower in carbohydrates than most.

¾   cup quinoa, rinsed, drained
2½   cups cold water
1   (8-oz.) carton unflavored (plain) yogurt
2   tablespoons chopped fresh dill
1   tablespoon chopped fresh curly parsley
2   teaspoons grated lemon peel
1   garlic clove, crushed
½   teaspoon salt
¼   teaspoon freshly ground pepper
2   cups (8 oz.) diced smoked chicken
4   cups mixed spring greens
2   avocados, peeled, halved
4   teaspoons very thinly sliced *Preserved Lemons* (page 38) (optional)

❶ In medium saucepan, cover quinoa with cold water. Bring to a boil; reduce heat to low. Simmer 10 to 15 minutes or until tender. Remove from heat; drain well.

❷ Meanwhile, in large bowl, combine yogurt, dill, parsley, lemon peel, garlic, salt and pepper. Add chicken and quinoa; toss well.

❸ Arrange greens on each of 4 salad plates. Top each plate with 1 avocado half. Pile quinoa mixture into avocado halves, spilling around edges of avocado. If desired, top each salad with Preserved Lemon slices.

4 servings.

Preparation time: 15 minutes. Ready to serve: 30 minutes.

Per serving: 400 calories, 18.5 g total fat (3.5 g saturated fat), 45 mg cholesterol, 575 mg sodium, 8.5 g fiber.

CORN AND BEAN SALAD

Like many bean salads, this colorful combination benefits from marinating in the refrigerator a few hours or even overnight. It teams up well with barbecued ribs and chicken.

1 cup dry white wine
1 jalapeño chile, halved*
¾ teaspoon salt
¼ teaspoon freshly ground pepper
¼ teaspoon ground cumin
¼ cup extra-virgin olive oil
2 cups (8 oz.) sugar snap peas, cut into 1-inch pieces
2 cups fresh corn kernels or 1 (16-oz.) can whole kernel corn, drained
1 (15-oz.) can cannellini (white) beans, drained, rinsed
2 tablespoons torn fresh basil
4 cups mixed spring greens
1 avocado, peeled, sliced
8 baby radishes, trimmed (use pink and white ones, if available)
36 tortilla chips

❶ In small skillet, combine wine and jalapeño. Bring to a boil. Reduce heat; simmer 10 minutes or until wine has reduced to ¼ cup. Set aside. Remove and discard jalapeño. Stir in salt, pepper and cumin; let cool. Whisk in olive oil.

❷ Meanwhile, heat heavy skillet over high heat until hot. Add peas and corn. Cook, stirring frequently, until peas and corn are toasted, about 3 minutes.

❸ In large bowl, combine peas, corn and white beans; toss. Add ¼ cup of the reduced wine dressing and basil; toss well.

❹ In large bowl, combine greens and remaining dressing; toss. Divide among 4 salad plates. Top each plate with 1 cup bean mixture. Garnish with avocado slices, radishes and tortilla chips.

4 (1-cup) servings.

Preparation time: 20 minutes. Ready to serve: 30 minutes.

Per serving: 480 calories, 24.5 g total fat (3.5 g saturated fat), 0 mg cholesterol, 775 mg sodium, 13.5 g fiber.

TIP *Crushed red pepper can be substituted for the jalapeño chile. Use ½ to 1 teaspoon.

CURRIED PILAF SALAD

While this dish resembles a hot rice pilaf, it makes a delicious salad when served chilled or at room temperature. For the best flavor, choose a good quality curry powder. To avoid overcooking the rice, test a few grains after about 15 minutes of cooking. For salads, the rice should be just a bit chewy.

1 tablespoon vegetable oil
½ cup finely chopped onion
2 garlic cloves, minced
1 tablespoon curry powder
1 cup basmati or long-grain white rice, rinsed, drained
1 (15 ½-oz.) can chicken broth (about 2 cups)
½ teaspoon salt
1 cup pitted dates, chopped
¼ cup finely chopped fresh curly parsley
¼ cup toasted pine nuts or slivered almonds

❶ In heavy 3-quart saucepan, heat oil over medium-high heat until hot. Add onion; cook, stirring constantly, 3 minutes. Add garlic and curry powder; cook, stirring constantly, 1 minute or until onion is tender and curry is fragrant.

❷ Stir in rice. Cook, stirring constantly, 1 minute. Stir in broth and salt; bring to a simmer. Reduce heat to medium-low. Simmer, covered, 20 to 30 minutes or just until rice is tender and liquid is absorbed.

❸ Transfer rice mixture to large bowl. Using large wooden spoon, gently stir and toss to cool. Stir in dates, parsley and pine nuts. Let cool to room temperature. (Salad can be prepared up to 24 hours ahead. Cover and refrigerate; bring to room temperature before serving.)

6 (1-cup) servings.

Preparation time: 20 minutes. Ready to serve: 50 minutes.

Per serving: 275 calories, 6.5 g total fat (1 g saturated fat), 0 mg cholesterol, 515 mg sodium, 4 g fiber.

CHEF'S NOTE
• For an entrée salad, stir in 1 cup diced, cooked turkey or chicken. Serve on bed of greens.

WARM FLAGEOLET SALAD WITH GRILLED SALMON

Flageolets (tiny pale green and white beans) can usually be found dried in specialty markets. Their delicate texture and flavor call for a light hand with seasoning. This recipe makes a beautiful al fresco summer dinner.

1	cup (½ lb.) dry flageolets, soaked 1 hour in hot water, drained and rinsed
2	tablespoons minced shallots
1	tablespoon fresh lemon thyme or regular thyme
1⅛	teaspoons salt
¼	plus ⅛ teaspoon freshly ground pepper
¼	cup Champagne vinegar or Chardonnay vinegar
⅓	cup plus 2 tablespoons extra-virgin olive oil
4	salmon fillets
4	generous slices herbed goat cheese

❶ In medium saucepan, cover flageolets with cold water. Bring to a simmer over medium-high heat; reduce heat to low. Simmer, partially covered, 30 minutes or until tender but not broken.

❷ In small bowl, combine shallots, thyme, 1 teaspoon of the salt, ¼ teaspoon of the pepper and vinegar. Whisk in ⅓ cup of the olive oil. Reserve ¼ cup of the dressing; pour remaining dressing over warm beans. (Beans can be prepared up to 24 hours ahead. Cover and refrigerate; bring to room temperature before serving.)

❸ Heat grill. Lightly brush salmon with remaining 2 tablespoons olive oil; sprinkle with remaining ⅛ teaspoon salt and ⅛ teaspoon pepper.

❹ Place salmon on gas grill over medium heat or on charcoal grill 4 to 6 inches from medium-hot coals. Cover grill; cook, turning once, 8 to 10 minutes or until fish just begins to flake.

❺ To serve, divide beans among 4 dinner plates. Top each with 1 fillet. Drizzle each with 1 tablespoon reserved dressing. Top each with 1 slice goat cheese.

4 servings.

Preparation time: 15 minutes. Ready to serve: 1 hour, 40 minutes.

Per serving: 630 calories, 35 g total fat (8.5 g saturated fat), 100 mg cholesterol, 800 mg sodium, 9 g fiber.

TABBOULEH

This is a take-off on traditional Tabbouleh, *with the added freshness of grapefruit. Use wedges of toasted pita bread to scoop up the salad.*

1 cup bulgur (cracked wheat)	¼ cup extra-virgin olive oil
¼ cup fresh mint, cut into thin ribbons	1 tablespoon fresh lemon juice
¼ cup finely chopped fresh curly parsley	¾ teaspoon salt
¼ cup finely chopped green onions	¼ teaspoon freshly ground pepper

PITA CRISPS

1 cucumber, peeled, seeded and diced	3 pita breads, split, cut into wedges
1 roasted red bell pepper, chopped	Olive oil spray
1 grapefruit, cut into sections	2 tablespoons zahtar (See TIP, page 131)
¼ cup grapefruit juice	1½ cups crumbled feta cheese

❶ In large bowl, cover bulgur with 1 quart boiling water. Let stand 30 minutes or until slightly chewy; drain.

❷ Stir in mint, parsley, green onions, cucumber, roasted pepper, grapefruit sections, grapefruit juice, olive oil, lemon juice, salt and pepper. Cover; refrigerate 1 to 4 hours.

❸ Thirty minutes before serving, heat oven to 400°F. Spray pita wedges with olive oil. Sprinkle with zahtar. Bake 5 to 8 minutes or until crisp.

❹ To serve, arrange 6 Pita Crisps around edge of each of 6 salad plates. Place about 1 cup Tabbouleh in center of pita wedges. Sprinkle each serving with ¼ cup feta cheese.

6 servings.

Preparation time: 40 minutes. Ready to serve: 1 hour, 40 minutes.

Per serving: 370 calories, 19.5 g total fat (7.5 g saturated fat), 35 mg cholesterol, 840 mg sodium, 6.5 g fiber.

PERFECT CITRUS SELECTIONS

Oranges, tangerines and grapefruit are all delicious and beautiful in salads. The most pleasant way to include citrus is with the thin membrane removed from each section. At first, this seems like a daunting task. But done correctly, it can be quick and yields lots of delicious juice.

Use a sharp knife to peel citrus fruit, cutting away all the white pulp and thin outer membrane. Holding the fruit over a bowl to catch the juice, cut between the fruit's inner membranes to loosen and remove segments.

THANKSGIVING SALAD

The nutty taste of brown and wild rice announces autumn. So it's natural to combine these grains with turkey and cranberries. To save time, prepare and assemble the other ingredients while the rice cooks.

¾ cup brown rice

½ cup wild rice

2½ cups cold water

1 cup dried cranberries

1 cup (5 oz.) diced smoked turkey

1 tablespoon cider vinegar

1 tablespoon hot mustard

½ teaspoon salt

¼ teaspoon freshly ground pepper

¼ cup extra-virgin olive oil

9 cups arugula or mustard greens

2 tablespoons walnut oil or hazelnut oil

❶ In medium saucepan, combine brown rice and wild rice. Add cold water. Bring to a boil; reduce heat to low. Simmer 45 minutes or until tender. Water should barely show bubbles as it simmers to prevent rice grains from breaking.

❷ Drain rice; transfer to large bowl. Gently toss to cool. Stir in cranberries, turkey, vinegar, mustard, salt, pepper and olive oil. Let cool to room temperature or cover and refrigerate. (Salad can be prepared up to 12 hours ahead. Cover and refrigerate; bring to room temperature before serving.)

❸ Place arugula in large bowl. Add walnut oil; toss to coat. Arrange about 1½ cups arugula on each of 6 salad plates. Top each with about ¾ cup rice mixture.

6 (¾-cup) servings.

Preparation time: 15 minutes. Ready to serve: 1 hour.

Per serving: 360 calories, 15.5 g total fat (2 g saturated fat), 10 mg cholesterol, 530 mg sodium, 3.5 g fiber.

LENTIL SALAD

Green and red lentils are beautiful but delicate. Cooking each color separately allows the red lentils to retain their bright orange color. You may also use all green or all red lentils.

¾ cup green lentils
¾ cup red lentils
1½ teaspoons salt
3 tablespoons grated onion
1 tomato, seeded, chopped
¼ cup chopped fresh Italian parsley
¼ cup extra-virgin olive oil
2 tablespoons sherry vinegar or red wine vinegar
1 tablespoon fresh thyme
¼ teaspoon freshly ground pepper
1 head butter lettuce, separated into leaves

❶ In small saucepan, cover green lentils with water. In another small saucepan, cover red lentils with water. Over medium-high heat, bring both to a simmer. Reduce heat to medium-low. Simmer, partially covered, 15 minutes. Add 1 teaspoon of the salt to each pan of lentils; cook an additional 5 minutes or just until lentils are tender but not broken. Drain; cool slightly.

❷ In large bowl, combine onion, tomato, parsley, olive oil, vinegar, thyme, remaining ½ teaspoon salt and pepper. Add warm lentils; gently toss. (Salad can be prepared up to 8 hours ahead. Cover and refrigerate; bring to room temperature before serving.)

❸ Arrange lettuce on 6 salad plates. Top each serving with about ½ cup lentil mixture.

6 (½-cup) servings.
Preparation time: 20 minutes. Ready to serve: 40 minutes.
Per serving: 250 calories, 9.5 g total fat (1.5 g saturated fat), 0 mg cholesterol, 395 mg sodium, 12 g fiber.

SANDWICH SALADS

Go beyond tuna salad sandwiches and explore new realms. The ingredient combinations in this chapter are fit for piling on top of greens, stuffing into tomatoes or making into a real and regal sandwich. Aim your sights on bakery-fresh pitas, crusty hearth-baked whole-grain bread, and spinach-green and beet-red tortillas. For big appetites, use big bread, such as salt- and herb-encrusted focaccia or submarine-size sourdough French rolls. These exciting sandwich holders turn soft white bread into yesterday's news.

Seasoned Steak
Salad Sandwich, page 134

123

CRAB LOUIS SANDWICH

Like Dungeness crab from which it's prepared, Crab Louis is a West Coast classic. Piled into sourdough rolls, Crab Louis becomes part salad and part sandwich.

¾ cup prepared *Mayonnaise* (page 48)
3 tablespoons bottled chili sauce
½ teaspoon Worcestershire sauce
3 tablespoons finely chopped green onions
2 tablespoons finely chopped green bell pepper
1 tablespoon fresh lemon juice
⅛ teaspoon salt
⅛ teaspoon freshly ground pepper
1 lb. fresh Dungeness crabmeat
4 sourdough rolls
2 cups shredded iceberg lettuce
2 small tomatoes, cut into wedges
2 tablespoons chopped fresh chives

❶ In small bowl, combine Mayonnaise, chili sauce, Worcestershire sauce, green onions, bell pepper, lemon juice, salt and pepper.

❷ Place crabmeat in large bowl. Add ½ cup of the dressing; gently toss without breaking up crabmeat.

❸ Cut each sourdough roll in half horizontally. Partially hollow each roll by removing some of the crumbs, leaving 1-inch-thick shell.

❹ Arrange ½ cup shredded lettuce on each of 4 salad plates. Top each with hollowed roll. Spoon about ½ cup crabmeat mixture into each roll. Tilt top of roll to the side.

❺ Arrange tomato wedges around roll; sprinkle with chives. Serve remaining dressing on the side.

4 sandwiches.

Preparation time: 20 minutes. Ready to serve: 30 minutes.

Per serving: 520 calories, 32 g total fat (4.5 g saturated fat), 155 mg cholesterol, 1045 mg sodium, 3 g fiber.

CURRIED TURKEY SALAD IN PITA BREADS

It's time to resurrect this '70s restaurant lunch favorite. Curried Turkey Salad *is creamy and luxurious when made with homemade* Mayonnaise. *To lighten up the recipe, replace half the Mayonnaise with low-fat sour cream or yogurt.*

1 tablespoon curry powder	¼ cup finely chopped celery
¾ cup prepared *Mayonnaise* (page 48)	6 cups mixed spring greens
2½ cups (12 oz.) diced smoked turkey	1 tablespoon extra-virgin olive oil
	⅛ teaspoon salt
2 cups small broccoli florets, blanched	⅛ teaspoon freshly ground pepper
	6 fresh pita breads, halved
½ cup golden raisins	⅓ cup toasted sliced almonds

❶ In small skillet, toast curry powder over medium heat until fragrant. Let cool. Stir into Mayonnaise.

❷ In large bowl, combine curry-mayonnaise mixture, turkey, broccoli, raisins and celery.

❸ In another large bowl, toss greens, olive oil, salt and pepper. Place ½ cup greens in each pita half. Spoon about ⅓ cup turkey mixture on top of greens. Sprinkle with almonds.

6 (⅔-cup) servings.

Preparation time: 15 minutes. Ready to serve: 20 minutes.

Per serving: 500 calories, 30 g total fat (4.5 g saturated fat), 150 mg cholesterol, 1205 mg sodium, 4.5 g fiber.

PESTO CHICKEN SALAD SANDWICHES

For a warm sandwich: Heat a stovetop grill pan. Omit the lettuce. Grill prepared sandwich until it's lightly golden on both sides and the cheese has just begun to melt.

- 2 cups shredded cooked chicken
- ½ cup prepared pesto*
- ½ cup chopped red bell pepper
- 2 cups curly green leaf lettuce
- 8 thin slices red onion
- 2 oz. sliced provolone cheese
- 4 squares (about 6x6-inch) focaccia bread, split in half horizontally, warmed

1. In medium bowl, combine chicken and pesto. Stir in bell pepper.

2. Layer lettuce, onion and cheese on bottom half of each focaccia square. Spread each with about ½ cup chicken mixture. Top with the other half focaccia. Cut each sandwich into halves, diagonally.

4 sandwiches.

Preparation time: 15 minutes. Ready to serve: 15 minutes.

Per serving: 910 calories, 45 g total fat (10 g saturated fat), 75 mg cholesterol, 1790 mg sodium, 5 g fiber.

TIP *Some prepared pesto is drier than others. If the chicken mixture appears dry, stir in about 1 tablespoon olive oil.

POACHED CHICKEN

Any leftover grilled, roasted or sautéed chicken is delicious when used in salads. But for the most tender and moist chicken of all, choose poached chicken. Here's how to poach:

Chicken Breasts. Place boneless skinless chicken breasts in a skillet. Add cold water to cover. Cover skillet and bring to a boil over medium heat. Reduce heat to low; simmer 10 minutes or until chicken juices run clear and internal temperature reaches 175°F to 180°F. Let cool. Shred chicken.

Bone-in Breasts. Simmer chicken 15 to 20 minutes or until chicken juices run clear and internal temperature reaches 175°F to 180°F. Let cool. Remove skin. Shred chicken.

Whole Chicken (about 3½ lb.). Place chicken in a large pot. Add a handful of parsley, a bay leaf and 1 rib of celery. Add water to cover. Bring to a boil over medium-high heat. Reduce heat to low. Simmer 25 to 30 minutes or until chicken juices run clear and internal temperature reaches 175°F to 180°F. Let cool. Remove skin. Shred chicken.

FRESH TUNA SALAD

Turn tuna salad up a notch by making it with freshly grilled fish. Serve this just as you'd serve canned tuna salad — in a tomato or avocado, on a bed of lettuce or between toasted pieces of good bread for a sandwich.

8 oz. tuna steak
¼ teaspoon salt
¼ teaspoon freshly ground pepper
⅔ cup prepared *Mayonnaise* (page 48)
2 tablespoons sour cream
1 tablespoon chopped fresh tarragon
2 teaspoons white wine vinegar
1 cup fresh peas or 1 cup (4 oz.) chopped sugar snap peas
2 tablespoons finely chopped red onion
4 beefsteak tomatoes, cut into quarters but connected at the bottom to open out, or 8 slices toasted sourdough bread
2 cups mixed spring greens

❶ Heat grill or broiler. Sprinkle tuna with salt and pepper. Cook 4 to 6 inches from heat, turning once, 8 to 10 minutes or until tuna is browned and just begins to flake. Let cool.

❷ In small bowl, combine Mayonnaise, sour cream, tarragon and vinegar. Stir in peas and onion. Flake tuna; fold into mayonnaise mixture.

❸ Pile about ½ cup tuna salad into center of each tomato. Place on plates lined with greens.

❹ To make sandwiches: Place about ½ cup greens on each of 4 slices of sourdough toast. Top each with about ½ cup tuna salad; top with remaining toast.

4 servings.

Preparation time: 15 minutes. Ready to serve: 25 minutes.

Per serving: 370 calories, 30 g total fat (5.5 g saturated fat), 55 mg cholesterol, 310 mg sodium, 4 g fiber.

CHEF'S NOTE
• One lb. fresh peas in the shell will yield about 1 cup shelled.

$\mathcal{S}$ALMAGUNDI SANDWICH

Salmagundi *is a made-up word referring to a salad containing everything but the kitchen sink! Originally a composed salad, the ingredients here blend well together to create a filling for an impressive sandwich.*

½ cup *Basic Vinaigrette* (page 43)
4 teaspoons prepared horseradish
2 cups shredded roasted or grilled chicken
½ cup chopped green beans, blanched
½ cup chopped red apple
¼ cup finely chopped yellow or green bell pepper
2 tablespoons drained capers
8 slices sourdough bread, toasted
2 hard-cooked eggs, whites chopped, yolks crumbled
1 tomato, seeded, diced

❶ In large bowl, combine Basic Vinaigrette and horseradish. Stir in chicken, beans, apple, bell pepper and capers.

❷ Pile ½ cup chicken mixture on each of 4 slices toast. Top each with 1 tablespoon egg and 2 tablespoons diced tomato. Top with remaining toast slices. Cut each sandwich into halves.

4 sandwiches.

Preparation time: 20 minutes. Ready to serve: 20 minutes.

Per serving: 440 calories, 20 g total fat (4 g saturated fat), 165 mg cholesterol, 730 mg sodium, 3 g fiber.

CHEF'S NOTE

• For perfect hard-cooked eggs, place eggs in a saucepan and cover with cold water. Bring to a boil. Cover and turn off heat. Let stand 10 minutes, then drain. Plunge eggs into cold water until cold. Very fresh eggs are the most difficult to peel.

SMOKY EGGPLANT SALAD

Middle Eastern salads are similar to our versions of dips and spreads. They make wonderfully flavorful sandwich fillings. Use smooth, heavy eggplants here. This ensures they are fresh and have more pulp and fewer seeds.

2   globe eggplants, about 1 lb. each
3   tablespoons extra-virgin olive oil
4   teaspoons zahtar*
2   teaspoons grated lemon peel
4   teaspoons fresh lemon juice
2   garlic cloves, crushed
¾   teaspoon salt
⅓   cup chopped fresh Italian parsley
6   fresh pita breads, quartered or halved, warmed

❶ Heat grill or broiler. Cook eggplant 6 inches from heat, turning as each side chars, until soft and charred on all sides. Let cool; peel. Place pulp in blender. Cover; pulse gently just until well chopped, not smooth.

❷ Transfer eggplant to medium bowl. Stir in olive oil, zahtar, lemon peel, lemon juice, garlic and salt. Sprinkle with parsley. Let sit at room temperature at least 1 hour before serving. (Salad can be prepared up to 24 hours ahead. Cover and refrigerate; bring to room temperature before serving.)

❸ To serve as an appetizer, place warm pita bread in napkin-lined basket. Serve with eggplant salad. To serve as a sandwich, spoon eggplant salad into pita bread halves. Sprinkle filling with parsley.

6 (⅓-cup) servings.

Preparation time: 30 minutes. Ready to serve: 1 hour, 30 minutes.

Per serving: 225 calories, 8 g total fat (1 g saturated fat), 0 mg cholesterol, 540 mg sodium, 4.5 g fiber.

TIP *Zahtar is a favorite spice mixture in Middle Eastern cuisines. To make your own, combine 1 tablespoon dried thyme, 1 tablespoon toasted sesame seeds and ¼ teaspoon ground sumac. Sumac is deep red and slightly tart. Both zahtar and sumac can be found in Middle Eastern markets.

VEGGIE SALAD WRAP

Shredded vegetable salads, such as coleslaw, are terrific accompaniments to sandwiches. But wrapped inside a tortilla, a Veggie Salad Wrap *becomes a hand-held lunch for folks on the go.*

½ cup prepared *Buttermilk Dressing* (page 42)
1 tablespoon chopped fresh oregano
1 teaspoon fresh thyme
⅛ teaspoon salt
⅛ teaspoon freshly ground pepper
1 carrot, shredded
1 zucchini, shredded
½ green bell pepper, finely chopped
1 cup iceberg lettuce, shredded
4 (8-inch) flour tortillas (use colorful tortillas, if available)
   Hot pepper sauce (optional)

❶ In small bowl, combine Buttermilk Dressing, oregano, thyme, salt and ground pepper.

❷ In large bowl, combine carrot, zucchini, bell pepper and lettuce. Stir in dressing; toss.

❸ Place about ½ cup vegetable mixture on each tortilla. If desired, sprinkle with hot pepper sauce. Roll up; serve seam-side down. If it's to be enjoyed on the go, wrap in aluminum foil.

4 wraps.

Preparation time: 15 minutes. Ready to serve: 20 minutes.

Per serving: 230 calories, 10 g total fat (1.5 g saturated fat), 0 mg cholesterol, 345 mg sodium, 3 g fiber.

CHEF'S NOTE

• It may seem that there is not enough dressing here to coat the vegetables. However, the vegetables quickly add their own moisture.

HEARTS OF PALM ON NINE-GRAIN TOAST

Despite the addition of a little cayenne pepper, this is a mild salad that lets the flavor of hearts of palm shine through.

½ cup prepared *Mayonnaise* (page 48)
¼ cup crumbled blue cheese
⅛ teaspoon cayenne pepper
1 (14-oz.) can hearts of palm, drained, chopped
1 cup seeded, finely chopped tomato
¼ cup finely chopped celery
8 slices nine-grain bread, toasted
2 cups watercress, large stems removed

❶ In medium bowl, combine Mayonnaise, blue cheese and cayenne.

❷ In large bowl, combine hearts of palm, tomato and celery. Add mayonnaise mixture; toss gently to mix well.

❸ Top 4 slices of nine-grain toast with ½ cup watercress. Top each serving with about ½ cup hearts of palm mixture and second slice of toast.

4 sandwiches.

Preparation time: 10 minutes. Ready to serve: 10 minutes.

Per serving: 355 calories, 23.5 g total fat (4.5 g saturated fat), 30 mg cholesterol, 810 mg sodium, 6.5 g fiber.

SEASONED STEAK SALAD SANDWICH

Served in a salad or on a sandwich, perfectly seasoned and cooked beef satisfies any hearty appetite. Top round steak is one of the leanest cuts available. Cooked medium-rare, it will be moist and juicy.

1	teaspoon dried oregano
½	teaspoon salt
¼	teaspoon cayenne pepper
¼	teaspoon freshly ground pepper
1	lb. top round steak
¼	cup apple juice concentrate
2	tablespoons red wine vinegar
1	tablespoon finely chopped fresh parsley
1	tablespoon finely chopped fresh oregano
1	cup chopped tart green apple
4	slices rye bread, toasted
2	tablespoons sweet hot mustard
2	cups baby arugula

❶ Heat grill or broiler. In small bowl, combine dried oregano, salt, cayenne and ground pepper. Season steak on both sides with oregano mixture. Cook steak 4 to 6 inches from heat, turning once, 10 minutes or until medium-rare. Let stand 10 minutes.

❷ Meanwhile, in large bowl, combine apple juice concentrate, vinegar, parsley and fresh oregano. Stir in green apple. Cut steak into thin slices. Stir into apple mixture; toss to coat steak.

❸ Spread each slice of toast with mustard; place on luncheon plate. Top each slice with ½ cup arugula and ¾ cup steak mixture.

4 sandwiches.

Preparation time: 15 minutes. Ready to serve: 25 minutes.

Per serving: 255 calories, 5 g total fat (1.5 g saturated fat), 60 mg cholesterol, 590 mg sodium, 3 g fiber.

FRUIT & DESSERT SALADS

Fruit and dessert salads are the coolest! Fresh, chilled fruit is refreshing any time of day, for any meal. The following recipes run the gamut from a banana split for breakfast to Fresh and Dried Fruit Salad *(page 139)* over ice cream in front of late-night TV. Spicy, tart and savory ingredients combine with fruit in pleasantly surprising ways. When the sweet tooth hits, knock it out with fresh fruit all dressed up!

Watermelon Salad, page 149

GRILLED APPLE AND RED ONION SALAD

If you thought comfort food and salads were two different things, think again. Grilled apples and onions with warming sage and ginger will make you change your mind. This salad is perfect with pork loin or lamb chops.

3	tablespoons cider vinegar
2	tablespoons chopped fresh sage
1	tablespoon grated fresh ginger
½	teaspoon salt
¼	teaspoon freshly ground pepper
3	tablespoons walnut oil
3	tablespoons extra-virgin olive oil
2	crisp red apples, cored, cut crosswise into ¼-inch-thick slices
1	large red onion, cut crosswise into ¼-inch-thick slices
3	cups torn red leaf lettuce
3	cups torn green leaf lettuce
⅓	cup chopped toasted walnuts

❶ In large bowl, combine vinegar, 1 tablespoon of the sage, ginger, salt and pepper. Whisk in walnut and olive oils.

❷ Heat stovetop grill pan or broiler. Brush apple and onion slices with ¼ cup of the dressing. Cook 5 minutes or until slightly tender, turning once during cooking. Separate onion into rings.

❸ In medium bowl, combine apples, onions and remaining dressing; gently toss.

❹ Arrange red and green leaf lettuce on each of 4 salad plates. Top each with apple slices and onion rings. Sprinkle salads with walnuts and remaining tablespoon sage.

4 servings.

Preparation time: 30 minutes. Ready to serve: 30 minutes.

Per serving: 315 calories, 25 g total fat (3 g saturated fat), 0 mg cholesterol, 300 mg sodium, 4.5 g fiber.

CHEF'S NOTE

• To core an apple and not waste any fruit, cut an apple in half. Using a melon ball scoop or metal ½ teaspoon, scoop out the seeds and stem.

FRESH AND DRIED FRUIT SALAD

Part fruit salad and part compote, this high-energy bowl of fruit is welcome any time of the day. Top it with yogurt for breakfast or serve it with a cookie for dessert. On the savory side, it makes an excellent relish for grilled chicken or chops.

½ cup dried apricots
½ cup dried plums (prunes)
½ cup dried cranberries
¾ cup fresh orange juice
3 tablespoons honey
3 tablespoons fresh lemon juice

2 teaspoons grated fresh ginger
2 tablespoons orange-flavored liqueur (optional)
2 fresh peaches, cut into wedges
1 pint halved strawberries
1 cup fresh blueberries

❶ In medium saucepan, combine dried apricots, dried plums, dried cranberries, orange juice, honey, lemon juice and ginger. Bring to a boil over medium-high heat, then reduce heat to low. Simmer 10 minutes or until fruit is slightly tender. If desired, stir in liqueur.

❷ Place peaches, strawberries and blueberries in serving bowl. Pour cooked fruit mixture over fresh fruit; stir. Let stand 1 hour to allow flavors to blend.

6 (¾-cup) servings.

Preparation time: 10 minutes. Ready to serve: 1 hour, 10 minutes.

Per serving: 185 calories, 0.5 g total fat (0 g saturated fat), 0 mg cholesterol, 10 mg sodium, 5 g fiber.

FENNEL AND PEAR SALAD

This fresh-tasting salad is perfect after a heavy entrée. To prevent fennel and pear slices from browning, immediately toss them with rice vinegar. You may refrigerate the salads for an hour or two, but add the blue cheese just before serving.

½ bulb fennel, trimmed just below green stems and above root end, cut into quarters

2 crisp red pears, halved, cored

3 tablespoons seasoned rice vinegar

1 tablespoon hazelnut oil or walnut oil

⅛ teaspoon salt

⅛ teaspoon freshly ground pepper

1 head butter lettuce, separated into leaves

¼ cup (2 oz.) crumbled blue cheese

❶ Using mandoline or very sharp knife, cut fennel into paper-thin slices. Place in large bowl.

❷ Quarter pears; cut into very thin, lengthwise slices. Add pears and vinegar to fennel; gently toss. Add oil, salt and pepper; toss again.

❸ Arrange lettuce on 4 salad plates. Top with fennel and pear slices. Sprinkle with blue cheese.

4 (½-cup) servings.

Preparation time: 15 minutes. Ready to serve: 15 minutes.

Per serving: 125 calories, 6.5 g total fat (2 g saturated fat), 5 mg cholesterol, 205 mg sodium, 3.5 g fiber.

CHEF'S NOTE

• To create lovely pear slices, cut a pear into halves, lengthwise. Remove the core using melon ball scoop or grapefruit spoon. Gently pull away the stem.

TROPICAL FRUIT SALAD

Sweet, spicy and tart come together in this peak-of-the-season fruit salad. Take a big bowl of colorful fruit to your next summer potluck; this recipe is easy to double.

MANGO POPPY SEED DRESSING

- 2 ripe mangoes, peeled, pitted
- ½ cup fresh orange juice
- 1½ teaspoons grated fresh ginger
- 1 teaspoon soy sauce
  Dash salt
- 1 tablespoon poppy seeds

FRUIT SALAD

- 2 kiwi fruit, peeled, sliced
- 1 cup strawberries, hulled, halved
- 1 small papaya, peeled, seeded and cut into ½-inch-thick slices
- ½ cup Maui, Vidalia or other sweet onion, chopped
- ½ cup sweetened coconut, toasted*

❶ In blender, combine 1 of the mangoes, orange juice, ginger, soy sauce and salt. Cover; blend until smooth. Pour into bowl; stir in poppy seeds.

❷ Cut remaining mango lengthwise into ½-inch-thick slices. In large bowl, combine mango slices, kiwi fruit, strawberries, papaya, onion and coconut; toss. Just before serving, add dressing and toss again.

6 (1-cup) servings.

Preparation time: 30 minutes. Ready to serve: 45 minutes.

Per serving: 130 calories, 3.5 g total fat (2 g saturated fat), 0 mg cholesterol, 125 mg sodium, 4 g fiber.

TIP *To toast coconut, heat oven to 350°F. Spread coconut on baking sheet and bake about 10 minutes, stirring occasionally, until crisp and lightly browned.

FUYU PERSIMMON SALAD

Persimmons are available only from about Halloween to New Year. Unlike the Hachiya, the Fuyu persimmon is delightful to eat while still firm. Peeled and sliced Fuyus need little embellishment. The simple vinaigrette here is a perfect complement.

VINAIGRETTE
- ½ cup white wine
- 1 vanilla bean, split to expose seeds
- ½ teaspoon salt
- ½ teaspoon freshly ground pepper
- 2 tablespoons hazelnut oil

SALAD
- 2 firm Fuyu persimmons, very thinly sliced

❶ In small saucepan, heat wine and vanilla bean until slowly simmering. Simmer 10 minutes or until wine has reduced to ¼ cup. Whisk in salt and pepper. Let cool. Remove vanilla bean. Scrape seeds into wine mixture; discard pod. Whisk in oil.

❷ Arrange persimmons on salad plates or on platter. Drizzle with vanilla vinaigrette.

4 servings (½ persimmon per serving).

Preparation time: 10 minutes. Ready to serve: 10 minutes.

Per serving: 125 calories, 7 g total fat (0.5 g saturated fat), 0 mg cholesterol, 150 mg sodium, 3 g fiber.

PLUM GELATIN SALAD

Fresh plums take gelatin salad to a whole new realm. This salad is best served on a dinner plate alongside a chop or roasted chicken. Add sugar only if the plums are not perfectly sweet.

1½	lb. fresh, very ripe plums, pitted
½	cup apple juice or water
1	tablespoon fresh lemon juice
½	teaspoon ground ginger
½	teaspoon ground cinnamon
½	teaspoon ground nutmeg
2	to 4 tablespoons sugar (depending upon sweetness of plums)
1½	(¼-oz.) envelopes unflavored gelatin (about 1 tablespoon)
¼	cup Maui, Vidalia or other sweet onion, minced
¾	cup chopped toasted walnuts

❶ In blender, combine plums, apple juice, lemon juice, ginger, cinnamon and nutmeg. Cover; blend until smooth. Add sugar to taste. Cover; blend until sugar is combined.

❷ Pour plum mixture into medium saucepan. Sprinkle with gelatin; let stand 2 minutes.

❸ Over medium heat, cook plum mixture, stirring constantly, until sugar and gelatin have dissolved, about 5 minutes. Let cool.

❹ Refrigerate until slightly thickened, about 30 minutes. Stir in onion and walnuts. Refrigerate until set, 1 to 1½ hours.

6 (½-cup) servings.

Preparation time: 15 minutes. Ready to serve: 2 hours, 15 minutes.

Per serving: 190 calories, 10 g total fat (1 g saturated fat), 0 mg cholesterol, 5.5 mg sodium, 2.5 g fiber.

CHEF'S NOTE

• For a dessert salad, increase sugar to ¾ cup and omit onions. Serve with softly whipped cream.

FRUIT-FILLED BANANA SPLITS

Finally — healthy banana splits! Don't say the word "salad" and the kids will crave these for after-school snacks. On the weekends, Fruit-Filled Banana Splits will keep you in top form as an after-workout breakfast.

1 (12-oz.) pkg. frozen raspberries, thawed	1 cup vanilla-flavored yogurt
½ cup orange juice	4 bananas
2 tablespoons sugar	1 cup fresh blueberries
1 (¼-oz.) envelope unflavored gelatin	1 cup granola or toasted walnuts

❶ Strain raspberries into medium bowl, pressing gently to release all juice. (Straining should yield about ¾ cup juice.) In small saucepan, combine raspberry juice, orange juice and sugar. Sprinkle with gelatin; let stand 2 minutes.

❷ Over medium-low heat, stir raspberry mixture until gelatin is dissolved, about 1 minute. Remove from heat; let cool 5 minutes. Whisk in yogurt until smooth. Spoon into medium bowl; refrigerate until firm, 1½ to 2 hours.

❸ Peel bananas; halve lengthwise. Place 2 banana halves on dessert plate or in banana split dish. Top each banana with about ½ cup raspberry mousse. Sprinkle with blueberries and granola. Serve immediately.

4 servings.

Preparation time: 15 minutes. Ready to serve: 2 hours, 15 minutes.

Per serving: 375 calories, 7.5 g total fat (4.5 g saturated fat), 5 mg cholesterol, 55 mg sodium, 9 g fiber.

$\mathcal{M}$ELON SALAD WITH SAFFRON CREAM

Slightly sweet and aromatic, this rich saffron cream topping is a luxurious addition to fresh fruit. The combination of saffron, pistachio nuts and honey is an ancient one worth remembering.

SALAD
- 2 cups cubed honeydew melon
- 2 cups cubed seedless watermelon
- 2 cups cubed fresh pineapple
- 1 tablespoon fresh lime juice

CREAM
- ¼ cup prepared *Mayonnaise* (page 48)
- 2 tablespoons honey
- ½ teaspoon (½ gram) saffron threads or ⅛ teaspoon powdered saffron
- ¾ cup heavy cream, whipped
- ¼ cup shelled chopped pistachio nuts

❶ In large bowl, combine honeydew, watermelon and pineapple. Sprinkle with lime juice; gently toss.

❷ In small bowl, combine Mayonnaise and honey. Crumble saffron threads; stir into mayonnaise mixture. Fold in whipped cream.

❸ Place 1 cup fruit on each of 6 salad plates. Top each serving with about 3 tablespoons saffron mixture; sprinkle with 2 teaspoons pistachios.

6 servings.

Preparation time: 30 minutes. Ready to serve: 30 minutes.

Per serving: 260 calories, 18.5 g total fat (7 g saturated fat), 40 mg cholesterol, 75 mg sodium, 1.5 g fiber.

WATERMELON SALAD

Cool, refreshing watermelon makes a fresh appearance as a salad here. Cumin, cilantro and lime lend a southwestern flavor, making Watermelon Salad *the perfect accompaniment to grilled chicken tacos and simmered black beans. Serve over watermelon wedges or other melon variations.*

LIME VINAIGRETTE
2 tablespoons fresh lime juice
½ teaspoon ground cumin
½ teaspoon crushed red pepper
¼ teaspoon salt
2 tablespoons olive oil

WATERMELON SALAD
2 slices (about 1-inch-thick) red, seedless watermelon
2 slices (about 1-inch-thick) yellow, seedless watermelon (or 2 additional slices red, seedless watermelon)
¼ cup fresh cilantro, torn

❶ In small bowl, combine lime juice, cumin, crushed red pepper and salt. Whisk in olive oil.

❷ Using sharp knife, trim rind from watermelon slices. Cut slices into 1-inch-wide strips.

❸ Arrange watermelon strips decoratively on each of 4 salad plates. Drizzle generously with dressing. Sprinkle with cilantro.

4 servings.

Preparation time: 20 minutes. Ready to serve: 20 minutes.

Per serving: 215 calories, 9 g total fat (1 g saturated fat), 0 mg cholesterol, 160 mg sodium, 2.5 g fiber.

$\mathcal{P}$ICNIC SALADS

When packing a picnic, remember to choose your meal carefully. Unless you are toting a good cooler packed with ice, you must avoid foods containing mayonnaise, fish and those all-time favorites, fried chicken and mayonnaise-based potato salad. Those foods are particularly vulnerable to spoilage on a warm summer day. Instead, try some of these delightful creations!

Lemon Coleslaw with Caraway Seeds, page 162

BLACK BEAN SALAD WITH CILANTRO PESTO

Canned, roasted green chiles work well in cilantro pesto, making this a quick salad to assemble. Add roasted chicken strips for a simple and healthy one-dish meal.

1   cup fresh chopped cilantro
¼   cup canned roasted green peppers, drained, rinsed (or ½ fresh green bell pepper, roasted and peeled)
1   tablespoon fresh lime juice
1   garlic clove, mashed
½   teaspoon salt
¼   cup extra-virgin olive oil
3   (15-oz.) cans black beans, rinsed and drained
1   cup cherry tomatoes, quartered
½   cup peeled, diced jicama
½   yellow bell pepper, cut into 1-inch strips
2   teaspoons fresh lime juice
2   teaspoons extra-virgin olive oil
½   teaspoon chili powder
     Tortilla chips, garnish

❶ In blender, combine cilantro, roasted pepper, 1 tablespoon lime juice, garlic and salt. Cover and blend until chunky. With blender running, add ¼ cup oil in a steady stream.

❷ In medium bowl, combine black beans and cilantro dressing. Toss to coat.

❸ In medium bowl, combine cherry tomatoes, jicama and yellow bell pepper. Add 2 teaspoons lime juice and 2 teaspoons olive oil; toss to coat. Spoon tomato mixture over beans. Sprinkle with chili powder.

❹ Just before serving, surround salad with tortilla chips.

6 (1-cup) servings.

Preparation time: 15 minutes. Ready to serve: 20 minutes

Per serving: 340 calories, 12.5 g total fat (2 g saturated fat), 0 mg cholesterol, 585 mg sodium, 12 g fiber.

RED, WHITE AND BLUE POTATO SALAD

Three different colors, textures and flavors! This fun potato salad is possible because of the growing interest in specialty produce. Shop local farmers' markets for these and other potato varieties.

1	lb. blue potatoes
½	lb. Yukon gold or creamer potatoes
½	lb. red potatoes
1	tablespoon salt
¼	tablespoon Champagne vinegar or white wine vinegar
2	tablespoons grated onion
1	teaspoon Dijon mustard
½	teaspoon salt
½	teaspoon freshly ground pepper
⅔	cup extra-virgin olive oil
2	tablespoons finely chopped oregano
1	tablespoon capers

❶ Place potatoes in large saucepan; add water to cover. Stir in 1 tablespoon salt. Bring to a boil over high heat; reduce heat to medium. Cook 20 minutes or until tender. Drain; let cool. Cut into quarters. Place in large bowl.

❷ In small bowl, combine vinegar, onion, mustard, ½ teaspoon salt and pepper; pour over potatoes; toss. Add olive oil, oregano and capers; gently toss again. Salad may be served slightly warm. (Salad can be prepared up to 24 hours ahead. Cover and refrigerate. Bring to room temperature before serving.)

8 (¾-cup) servings.

Preparation time: 40 minutes. Ready to serve: 50 minutes.

Per serving: 260 calories, 18 g total fat (2.5 g saturated fat), 0 mg cholesterol, 455 mg sodium, 2.5 g fiber.

CHEF'S NOTE
- If potatoes are uneven in size, cut larger potatoes. Potatoes should be tender all the way through when cooked, but not too soft.

PANZANELLA (ITALIAN BREAD SALAD)

Panzanella is like chili. Everyone who makes it has his or her own recipe, bread being the common denominator here. I enjoy Panzanella the most when it sits overnight and the bread soaks up all the flavor and becomes really moist.

6 slices coarse, hearth-baked bread, crusts removed, interior cubed
1 tablespoon capers
1 garlic clove
1 teaspoon anchovy paste or 2 anchovies
½ teaspoon salt
¼ teaspoon crushed red pepper
¼ cup extra-virgin olive oil
1 tablespoon balsamic vinegar
2 plum tomatoes, halved lengthwise, sliced
½ red onion, thinly sliced, soaked in ice water 5 minutes and drained
1 cucumber, peeled, halved lengthwise, seeded, sliced

❶ Layer ⅓ of the bread cubes in bottom of large bowl.

❷ Using a mortar and pestle or the side of a chef's knife, mash capers, garlic, anchovy paste, salt and red pepper into a paste; transfer to small bowl. Whisk in olive oil and balsamic vinegar.

❸ Place tomatoes in bowl, stir in oil mixture. Spoon about ⅓ of the tomato mixture over the bread cubes. Sprinkle tomato mixture with about ⅓ of the onion and ⅓ of the cucumber. Repeat layers until all ingredients are used.

❹ Cover and refrigerate at least 1 hour for flavors to blend. If desired, sprinkle with a little olive oil just before serving. (Salad can be prepared up to 24 hours ahead. Cover and refrigerate. Bring to room temperature before serving.)

8 (1-cup) servings.

Preparation time: 30 minutes. Ready to serve: 2 hours.

Per serving: 260 calories, 18 g total fat (2.5 g saturated fat), 0 mg cholesterol, 455 mg sodium, 2.5 g fiber.

CHINESE CABBAGE SALAD

Crinkly Chinese cabbage has a mild flavor and wonderful texture. This light, bright salad is delicious with rich barbecued food such as grilled teriyaki ribs.

1 head Chinese (napa) cabbage, cored, quartered lengthwise
2 ribs celery, thinly sliced (about 1½ cups)
1 carrot, shredded (about 1 cup)
½ cup chopped celery leaves, if available
¼ cup seasoned rice vinegar
1 tablespoon grated fresh ginger
1 tablespoon sesame oil
½ teaspoon salt
¼ teaspoon freshly ground white pepper

❶ In large bowl, combine cabbage, celery, carrot and celery leaves; toss.

❷ In small bowl, combine rice vinegar, ginger, sesame oil, salt and pepper. Toss with cabbage mixture. (Cabbage will lose volume when dressed.)

8 (¾-cup) servings.

Preparation time: 20 minutes. Ready to serve: 30 minutes.

Per serving: 40 calories, 2 g total fat (0 g saturated fat), 0 mg cholesterol, 230 mg sodium, 1.5 g fiber.

ROASTED VEGETABLE SALAD WITH CURRIED BALSAMIC VINAIGRETTE

Root vegetables take on a nutty flavor when they're roasted. Here, the spices are roasted into the vegetables for deep flavor and the salad is finished with a toss of balsamic vinegar and olive oil.

2 parsnips, peeled, each cut into 1-inch pieces

1 rutabaga, peeled, cut into 1-inch pieces

1 bulb fennel, trimmed just below the green stems and above the root end, cut into 1-inch pieces

12 garlic cloves, peeled, halved

2 teaspoons curry powder

1 teaspoon salt

½ teaspoon freshly ground pepper

2 tablespoons olive oil

3 portobello mushrooms, cut into 1-inch pieces

2 tablespoons balsamic vinegar

2 tablespoons extra-virgin olive oil

❶ Heat oven to 375°F. Spread parsnips, rutabaga, fennel and garlic evenly over baking sheet. Sprinkle with curry powder, salt and pepper; drizzle with olive oil. Stir vegetables to coat with oil mixture. Roast 15 minutes. Stir in mushrooms, cook an additional 15 minutes or until vegetables are tender.

❷ Transfer vegetables to large bowl. Sprinkle with balsamic vinegar; toss. Sprinkle with extra-virgin olive oil; toss again. Let sit at room temperature 1 hour for flavors to blend. (Salad can be prepared up to 24 hours ahead. Cover and refrigerate. Bring to room temperature before serving.)

6 (1-cup) servings.

Preparation time: 20 minutes. Ready to serve: 30 minutes.

Per serving: 170 calories, 9.5 g total fat (1 g saturated fat), 0 mg cholesterol, 425 mg sodium, 4.5 g fiber.

SWEET POTATO SALAD

This is potato salad elevated to a higher plane! When sweet potato slices are slowly roasted, they take on a creamy texture while still holding their shape. Roasted onions are a nutty-sweet treat.

2   lb. sweet potatoes, cut into ½-inch-thick slices
1   tablespoon olive oil
1   Maui, Vidalia or other sweet onion, cut into 1-inch cubes
1   tablespoon olive oil
2   tablespoons water
2   tablespoons extra-virgin olive oil
1   tablespoon fresh lemon juice
1   tablespoon balsamic vinegar
½   teaspoon freshly ground nutmeg
½   teaspoon salt
¼   teaspoon freshly ground pepper
2   tablespoons chopped Italian parsley

❶ Heat oven to 375°F. Evenly arrange sweet potato slices over baking sheet. Drizzle with 1 tablespoon olive oil. Stir potato slices to lightly coat with oil, leaving them in a single layer.

❷ Place onion pieces on another baking sheet. Drizzle with 1 tablespoon olive oil. Stir onions to lightly coat with oil, leaving them in a single layer. Bake potatoes and onions 30 minutes or until potatoes are slightly soft and onions are tender but not brown. Transfer potatoes to large bowl.

❸ In blender, combine onions, water, extra-virgin olive oil, lemon juice, vinegar, nutmeg, salt and pepper. Cover and blend until smooth. Pour over potatoes, toss. Add parsley, toss again.

6 (1-cup) servings.
Preparation time: 20 minutes. Ready to serve: 30 minutes.
Per serving: 185 calories, 9.5 g total fat (1 g saturated fat), 0 mg cholesterol, 205 mg sodium, 3.5 g fiber.

MARINATED BABY ARTICHOKES

The smallest artichokes are best for this recipe because they haven't developed the fuzzy choke. If destined for a picnic, place the Parmesan shavings in a plastic container and add just before serving.

1	lemon	¼	cup extra-virgin olive oil
12	baby artichokes	¼	cup pitted dry cured olives
¼	cup balsamic vinegar	2	tablespoons large capers
2	garlic cloves, crushed	2	tablespoons toasted pine nuts
½	teaspoon crushed red pepper	1	small wedge Parmesan or Pecorino cheese
½	teaspoon salt		
¼	teaspoon freshly ground black pepper		

❶ Grate lemon; reserve peel. Fill skillet with a lid about one-third full of water, add juice from lemon; stir.

❷ Cut the top quarter from each artichoke and remove outer leaves until the yellow leaves are visible. Using a paring knife or vegetable peeler, gently remove the dark green layer at the base of the artichokes and stems. Trim about ⅛ inch from the stem, cut the artichoke in half lengthwise, and add to skillet with lemon and water.

❸ Bring to a boil, reduce heat and simmer 20 to 30 minutes or until very tender. Transfer to glass or ceramic bowl.

❹ In small bowl, combine balsamic vinegar, garlic, red pepper, salt, black pepper and reserved lemon peel. Stir into artichokes. Stir in olive oil, olives, capers and pine nuts. Marinate 2 hours at room temperature. (Salad can be prepared up to 24 hours ahead. Cover and refrigerate. Bring to room temperature before serving.)

❺ Using a vegetable peeler, shave 8 large pieces Parmesan from the wedge. Just before serving, arrange Parmesan shavings over top of artichokes.

6 servings (4 artichoke halves per serving).

Preparation time: 25 minutes. Ready to serve: 2 hours, 30 minutes.

Per serving: 100 calories, 7 g total fat (0.5 g saturated fat), 0 mg cholesterol, 205 mg sodium, 1.5 g fiber.

CHEF'S NOTES

• If baby artichokes are unavailable, purchase the smallest artichokes you can find. Snap off all the thick, green leaves leaving only the tender yellow leaves. Using a paring knife or vegetable peeler, cut away the dark outer layer from the base and stems. Cut ½ inch from the stem and the dark top of the artichoke. Cut in quarters lengthwise. Using a paring knife or grapefruit spoon, scrape away the fuzzy choke. Proceed with step #3.

• Rather than wasting the thick outer leaves of artichokes, I like to steam them and eat them as a snack.

SPICED BEETS ON GREENS

Treat yourself to a new jar of mace. This sweet-tasting spice is the dried, ground outer covering of nutmeg seeds. The combination of mace and lemon balances wonderfully with roasted beets.

1 lb. beets, stems trimmed to 1 inch above beets
¼ cup diced onion, soaked in ice water 5 minutes and drained
1 tablespoon fresh lemon juice
¼ teaspoon ground mace
¼ teaspoon salt
2 tablespoons walnut oil or hazelnut oil
4 interior butter lettuce leaves

❶ Heat oven to 400°F. Place beets in casserole. Add ¼ cup water. Cover with aluminum foil. Bake 45 minutes to 1 hour or until tender.

❷ Cut stem and root from beets; peel. Cut into slices, then into thin strips. Transfer to bowl.

❸ Add onion, lemon juice, mace and salt to beets; toss. Add 1 tablespoon of walnut oil; toss again.

❹ Drizzle remaining walnut oil over lettuce leaves; toss. Arrange 1 leaf on each plate; top with beets.

4 (½-cup) servings
Preparation time: 15 minutes. Ready to serve: 1 hour.

Per serving: 100 calories, 7 g total fat (0.5 g saturated fat), 0 mg cholesterol, 205 mg sodium, 5.5 g fiber.

LEMON COLESLAW WITH CARAWAY SEEDS

Coleslaw is all about crunchy texture. For crisp cabbage, rinse it in very cold water; let it sit for a few minutes, then spin it dry with a salad spinner.

¼ medium red cabbage, shredded, rinsed and dried
¼ medium green cabbage, shredded, rinsed and dried
½ cup green onion
1 tablespoon caraway seeds
2 teaspoons grated lemon peel
2 tablespoons fresh lemon juice
½ teaspoon salt
⅛ teaspoon cayenne pepper
⅛ teaspoon ground white pepper
¼ cup extra-virgin olive oil

❶ In large bowl, combine red cabbage, green cabbage and green onion; toss.

❷ Sprinkle caraway seeds, lemon peel, lemon juice, salt, cayenne pepper and white pepper evenly over the top of the cabbage; toss. Add olive oil, toss again. (Salad can be prepared up to 12 hours ahead. Cover and refrigerate. Bring to room temperature before serving.) (Cabbage will lose volume when dressed.)

4 (1-cup) servings.

Preparation time: 10 minutes. Ready to serve: 20 minutes.

Per serving: 100 calories, 7 g total fat (0.5 g saturated fat), 0 mg cholesterol, 205 mg sodium, 5.5 g fiber.

RECIPE INDEX

This index lists every recipe in Splendid Salads *by name. If you're looking for a specific recipe but can't recall the exact name, turn to the General Index that starts on page 166.*

GENERAL INDEX

There are several ways to use this helpful index. First — you can find recipes by name. Second — if you don't know a recipe's specific name but recall a special ingredient or the type of salad, look under that heading and all the related recipes will be listed; scan for the recipe you want. Finally — you can use this general index to find a summary of recipes in each chapter of the book (green salads, vegetable salads, pasta salads, etc.).

RECIPE NOTES

RECIPE NOTES

RECIPE NOTES

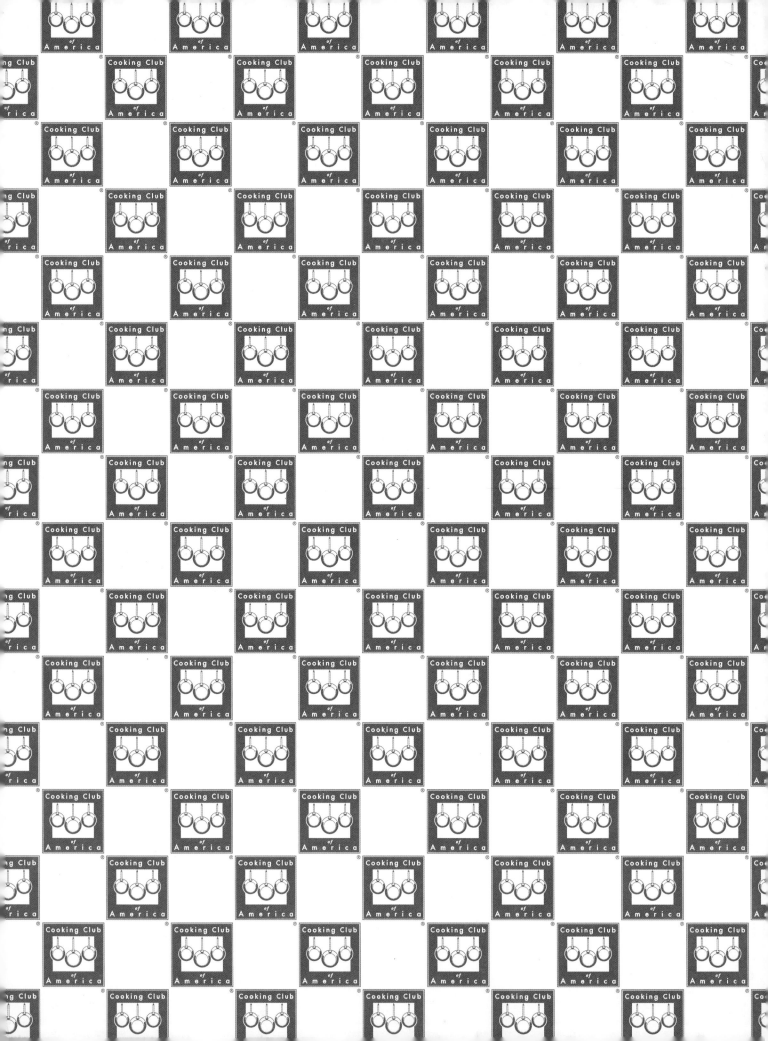